ON...

Geoff Birch

Foreword by Bryn Thomas

The
United
Reformed
Church

On... by Geoff Birch

ISBN 0 85346 249 6

© The United Reformed Church, 2006

Published by The United Reformed Church
86 Tavistock Place, London WC1H 9RT

Produced by Communications and Editorial, Graphics Office.

FOREWORD

You want to stimulate thinking.........

..... in a discussion group?
..... for a talk to interested adults?
..... with material for a youth group?
...... because you have been asked to take a secondary school assembly?
..... because you want a change from a lectionary-based sermon?

This book richly provides what you are looking for.

Some people have both information and imagination, and know how to express their thoughts without wasting a word. When the rest of us run dry of ideas, we turn to thought-provoking collections like this.

Geoff Birch sometimes says what I've always thought but haven't found a way of expressing; sometimes he grabs my attention because the thought has never crossed my mind. A successful senior schoolmaster, now retired, and an elder of the United Reformed Church, he has provided education in depth throughout his career: not just the facts but the values, not only information but inspiration also. The wealth of his experience and reflection shows through on every page.

Bryn Thomas

To my wife Hazel, for her encouragement,
her – occasionally unwitting – inspiration,
and above all for her unending patience.

CONTENTS

INTRODUCTION

One of the more important aspects of any teacher's work is that concerned with the by now vast industry of pastoral care. Teachers are not concerned only, or even mainly, with their academic specialities: most have duties as form tutors, some as heads of year; and some schools have a deputy head whose responsibilities are mainly pastoral. In my early years the form tutor was the kingpin of the system – that teacher was the first point of reference for the welfare of the children in the group, and was regarded by more traditionally-minded head teachers as the kingpin of the system. As our schools grew larger and more complex, so it was found necessary to appoint heads of year, heads of school, co-ordinators – and with every appointment so made, children found it more and more difficult to have themselves listened to by someone close to them. Now, as I understand it, we have re-invented the wheel by bringing back the form tutor. But what we do has not changed: we try to put across our values, our beliefs, our principles – all in the fond assumption that they are good and true.

But at the same time the responsibility for leading school assemblies has been diffused, to anyone willing and able to do so. That challenge was a great opportunity for teachers to exercise their pastoral responsibilities; but at the same time it was a challenge that not all teachers found it easy to accept. Some teachers, indeed, have a conscientious objection to taking such gatherings; and that is of course their right. But even teachers who find it difficult to take on this task are still putting across a point of view, an example, for their pupils to follow.

Every so often we should perhaps take a step backwards and review what we are doing and why. Until I retired I had been taking assemblies for more years that I care to think about: I presumed while I was still working to believe that my pupils found what I had to say useful, pertinent, even perhaps sometimes amusing. It is certainly presumptuous, that anyone should dare to stand in front of such a critical audience and try to put across something of importance; but then that is what teaching is all about. So why this particular activity?

Schools have – are required to have – a statement of "Aims and Objectives"; a horrible and in many ways meaningless phrase to describe our aspirations for our pupils. All schools have this in common: that they seem to want to send out into the world self-reliant, upstanding, reliable young people. Should we as teachers not also want to make them perceptive, critical, socially aware? So perhaps we should set out to make them think by what we say in front of them; perhaps even, especially as they grow older and more mature, it would be better to have them participate, discuss, argue with us; perhaps – later – they could be invited to take their own assemblies, to give their own views on what we have had to say to them. Whatever may be the case, however, they will leave school having willy-nilly absorbed some of our ideas and values. They may consciously reject what we say – do the opposite; but even in that way they are reflecting what we as teachers may think and do and say.

All the following are based very strongly on the short addresses which I have given over the years to my own pupils, both comprehensive and selective, and across the secondary age range. In that sense most of them have been "road-tested"; and a number of them have also been subjected to that most ferocious of critiques – from sixth formers in a grammar school. Very often the impetus for what I had to say was some event, in school, in the local community, or in the wider world; and – of course – events in the Christian calendar. In some cases my pupils would ask me to follow up what they had heard, while at the same time wishing to make their own contribution; and I nearly always found that the collective wisdom of pupils was by no means worthy only of being ignored. In some cases they came up with insights that I had missed – and which I then shamelessly incorporated into edited addresses. Each address can therefore be used simply as it stands, by teachers who are I know often hard pressed to find material for that weekly five-minute slot. But it is also quite possible to open up discussion, especially among older and more mature pupils. I have tried to suggest some "Points to Ponder" for each address – though in my experience pupils will always find their own questions to ask, given the right encouragement. In this way perhaps I and my colleagues – some of whose contributions have helped (anonymously) to influence this collection – were trying to put across a sense of our common Christian heritage. I say Christian, but non-Christians found a great deal of common ground, nothing to disagree with, a lot with which they felt in sympathy. I do not therefore feel any need to apologise for giving this collection a distinctly Christian bias.

That transmission of what might be termed "culture" is probably what Thucydides had in mind, when he wrote nearly two and a half millennia ago: "For the whole earth is the sepulchre of famous men, and their story is not only graven on stone over their native earth, but lives on far away, without visible symbol, woven into the stuff of other men's lives". Perhaps that is just one form of immortality – the continuity of civilisation: which incidentally we can never fully understand unless we are prepared to take an historical perspective. To see where we are coming from will enable us to see more clearly where we are going; to ignore it will inevitably lead to the repetition of old mistakes, the reinforcement of old prejudices.

In conclusion, if we are truly to set the pattern of what we would like our pupils to be, we could do much worse than recall the words of the Book of Common Prayer: "Go forth into the world in peace; be of good courage; hold fast that which is good; render to no man evil for evil; strengthen the faint-hearted; support the weak; help the afflicted; honour all men; love and serve the Lord, rejoicing in the power of the Holy Spirit; and the blessing of God Almighty, Father, Son and Holy Spirit, be upon you and remain with you for ever".

ON AMBITION

Ambition is, or can be, a marvellous thing. It can carry us onward and upward; or it can throw us down. The desire – the need, to do better is often the driving force behind improvement: that quality known as divine discontent which makes us critical of the status quo, makes us look for better things, or better ways of doing things. Teachers often need to instil a sense of ambition in their pupils, to open eyes to the boundless possibilities ahead, to make them aware of the ways in which they can do, or be, better. At the same time there is also the necessity sometimes to show that ambitions are unrealistic, and that aspirations need to fit abilities or situations. Such awareness sometimes comes with age and maturity. The American writer Henry Thoreau once wrote: "The Boy gathers materials for a Temple, and then when he is thirty concludes to build a Woodshed" – we plan for a glorious future, but as we grow older we realise that our plans are going nowhere, or at the very least that they are beyond us. In fact it does not matter all that much – provided that sights are not lowered too far: a friend of mine wanted to follow in his father's footsteps and become an optician; but had instead to reconcile himself to becoming an optical technician, a job at which he has in fact excelled.

But where should be the focus of our ambition? Should we be ambitious to be; or to have; or to do? In my time I have met many people who fell into that first category: they wanted the titles, without necessarily being able or willing to do what was needed to get there or to hold the job. When I was at school we called them "pot-hunters" – they wanted to stack one high-sounding position on another. In the same way, I suppose, we are now falling into the trap of using euphemisms: it is much "nicer" to be known as a salvage expert rather than a dustman; or a rodent operative rather than a rat-catcher. All too often those who seek these titles are quite happy to trample on others in their rush up the ladder of promotion: but Joseph Conrad wrote: "All ambitions are lawful except those which climb upward on the miseries or credulities of mankind". If we harbour ambitions of this sort, think of the anger and resentment and perhaps even jealousy which we may be storing up for ourselves.

Perhaps, however, we are ambitious to have: to own a fast flashy car, or the latest in computer technology, or a luxury flat; and then we need the ambition to find the job which will pay enough to satisfy these urges. The dangers here are even greater: we are reminded all too often that "You can't take it with you". Jesus had a parable for this – the story of the man who built huge barns to store his ever-growing wealth, and who was then visited by the Angel of the Lord, who told him that he was a fool, because the Lord would that very night require his soul – he would die. All his efforts to preserve his wealth were therefore useless.

Then again we might be ambitious to do – perhaps the best ambition of all, to do the best that we can, in whatever field that might be. But again there are dangers: are we working solely for ourselves? Are we working to be recognised, as an expert or as a hard-working member of the firm? Are we working to earn the praise of our peers? Or rather, are we working to better ourselves and our families? Or to better the lot of others less fortunate? Or to make discoveries or inventions for the benefit of all? Do not misunderstand me: as I said, ambition can be, and often is, a most positive force for progress; and without it we would none of us achieve as much as with it. And we all need to work for our own material benefit, for everyone needs to eat, needs clothing and shelter. We all benefit from the feeling of enjoying a certain status, within our families or in the wider world; and that feeling can often spur us to even greater endeavour. It is when we allow our ambitions to take us over that the dangers begin: Macbeth, in Shakespeare's great play, began with no ambitions for himself. Only when he gave way to the siren voice of his wife, and saw a higher, more glorious future for himself, did his troubles start. Keep a sense of proportion!

Points to Ponder

Do you fall into one or other of these categories?
Do you know others who do?
Do you see ambition as useful – positive; or injurious and harmful?

ON BEING A CHRISTIAN

S everal years ago the Minister of a Church I attended wrote of his worry that the Christian message seemed increasingly to be merely a question of morals or ethics or good-neighbourliness. He quoted a number of examples, notably where RE teachers in schools were proud that they never referred to the Bible in their teaching, but instead laid heavy emphasis solely on service and responsibility to the community. He pointed out that these aspects were of course important; but that they were not the sum total of Christian teaching.

When I read this I realised that my own efforts in the past – standing at the front talking about things which bother me, could be seen in this light. Do not mistake me: like that Minister, I believe that our attitudes towards each other are vitally important. But those attitudes are the outward signs of an inner conviction; they follow naturally from it. Seven hundred years before Christ, the prophet Micah wrote to sum up our duty: "For what doth the Lord require of thee, but to do justly, and to love mercy, and to walk humbly with thy God?" (6: 8). The first two are comparatively easy to understand for that is what we mean when we talk about "social attitudes"; but how do we "walk humbly with our God"? Who is God, what is He?

Reaching back far into pre-history, man as man became aware of, and was prepared to acknowledge, a power beyond himself; he looked for meaning and purpose in his existence; he looked for explanations of natural phenomena. In so doing he invoked all manner of gods, which, in the days before science as we know it, was perhaps quite rational; even if the ways in which he sought to worship and placate those gods was not so rational.

Back in the sixties, when I was a student, the Bishop of Woolwich and others encouraged us to seek God in our own being, thus putting a new slant on the old jibe about man making God in his own image. God was no longer to be sought "out there". So man has illusions of grandeur, of setting himself up as an equal of the Gods. The Greeks called it *hubris*; and it was always followed by *nemesis* – the terrible fate that befalls us for our temerity and insolence. Hence we must walk humbly; our cleverness does not make us wise. It is incidentally a view that Christians share with those of other faiths: within the Muslim world King Abdullah of Jordan once delivered this message to the Arab Legion:

> "In these days we see men who have created bombs and machines and electricity and other things, and who are so pleased with their own cleverness that they say there is no God. They hope that their inventions will save mankind. These men are clever, but they are not wise – the fear of God is the beginning of wisdom. Soldiers are nearer to death than other men, and it is essential for us to understand who we are. It is necessary for us to realise that God, not men, created the Universe, and only God, not men, can control it. We must not fall into the same errors as the Unbelievers and count up our guns, our bombs, our tanks and our aeroplanes and pray to them for deliverance. This is a new idolatry, like those who once worshipped stones and trees. Men have always lived and died, nations have risen and fallen, wars have come and gone. God alone is eternal, and rules life and death, victory and defeat. All that we soldiers have to do is to do our duty to God, to the King and to the Nation. Let us remember, for the rest, that God created the World and He rules it alone."

God, I think, *is* within us. We talk of the divine spark which impels us to greater things: to become not gods, but fuller human beings as we become aware of the powers within us. That is, I know, the humanist approach; but so far there is nothing which is incompatible with the Christian message. God is still something else, beyond ourselves. His existence cannot be proved as can science: it has to be taken on trust, ie faith. We believe, and act accordingly. We "do justly and love mercy". As our awareness grows, so we recognise the workings of a superior intelligence.

Twice in the past I have deliberately disrupted my life to change its course. On both occasions I laid my plans very carefully – and they came to nothing. With the benefit of hindsight I can see that what actually happened was probably better for me. Certainly I became aware of what you might call a guardian angel. And I have seen, on numerous occasions, prayer answered, prayers for strength of will, for the recovery of a near and dear one, or for wisdom and insight. All that has strengthened my own conviction and faith. Hence, I am a Christian.

Points to Ponder

Is any religious faith these days justified?

Is it possible to be a truly good person without a faith?

Few people really choose a faith. Instead they take that of their parents or of their society. Does it matter?

Does it make sense to leave things to God?

ON CHALLENGE

Those who have been "privileged" enough to come under my influence soon knew that I never sought to make life easy for them. Some had the temerity to complain that I seemed to go out of my way to make difficulties – which I took as a compliment. Many probably asked themselves why.

Psychologists tell us that we learn more effectively those things where a little effort is needed; another psychologist found that half-completed tasks were also better remembered and understood than those which we had finished, and therefore discarded. As a crossword fanatic I find often that a word to finish the puzzle often escapes me; but then it will come to me while I am otherwise occupied – my brain has been working at it subconsciously. There is a saying: "I hear and I forget; I see and I remember; I do and I understand". The job of a teachers is not so much to give the answers, or perhaps even to show how to arrive at them, as to equip pupils to find them for themselves. The efforts involved in the processes of trial-and-error, and of both linear and lateral thinking, are more efficient in helping us to learn. I remember my first deputy headmaster coming into lunch one day after a particularly difficult sixth-form lesson, exclaiming: "I wish that someone would write a book called *Mathematics made difficult!*" He had found what many teachers discover, that if things are explained too easily then the point is missed and there will be no effort made to understand how the conclusion is reached.

But there is more to it than that. When I was a boy myself, I was lucky in having a schoolmaster, and a Scout leader, who were likewise inclined. They put obstacles in our way, physical and intellectual, in the hope that we would accept the challenge, and find a way over the obstacle or a way of removing it. We were discouraged from ever simply turning our backs on the challenges offered. At first it was a game: could we outwit our elders in quite trivial matters? And we learned that we could – though with the benefit of hindsight we could see that these games were just that – artificially devised games. As time went on we grew used to the idea of pitting our wits against these artificial barriers. Then as we grew older ourselves, we came up against barriers which were *not* deliberately placed: no-one had been at work to hinder us, they had arisen simply through circumstance. By then we had become rather more used to the idea of facing challenge; and we were, it was hoped, strong enough to accept these new difficulties and to overcome them. What had originally been something of a game was by then second nature: never fail to rise to a challenge. I hope and believe that many of those I taught did see this as a game; for after all there is nothing more satisfying than to feel that you have outwitted your teachers! And I will have also done what I set out to do – to make them think.

Abraham Lincoln had a few pithy words to say on the same subject: "A river becomes crooked by following the line of least resistance. So does a man." These barriers which we raise against pupils are part of that function which we have as teachers: if we can show them how to tackle difficulties, with integrity and strength of purpose, and how to enjoy the sense of personal satisfaction which will surely ensue, then following the line of least resistance will simply not occur to them. Life, after all, is a challenge, the greatest of all.

Points to Ponder

Is life too easy for people these days?
Do young people in particular stagnate if not challenged?
Will they then seek their own "challenges" in anti-social behaviour?

ON CHRISTMAS

At Christmas our thoughts naturally turn to planning for presents, for a season of over-eating and over-drinking, a time of general jollification. It has always, from time immemorial, been the custom to celebrate the turn of the sun, just after the shortest day, by such merry-making, possibly as a means of lightening the otherwise unmitigated gloom of a European winter. It was also the symbol and the opportunity for a new beginning, the chance to put the old year behind us, and to look with hope to the new. It was no accident that the early Christians took over the festival and gave it a new significance. For too many people the season of Christmas is no more than one of merry-making: the essential message of the "still small voice" is too often drowned out by the clamour and clangour of our over-commercialised feast. For a few, however, there is all the magic and mystery of a free, unconditional, God-given present, mirrored by the gifts which the three Wise Men brought with them on their long pilgrimage. Those gifts too had their own symbolism: gold to signify Christ's kingship; frankincense to signify His priesthood; and myrrh – a sort of herb used in funeral rites – which pointed the way to Christ's eventual horrible death on Good Friday. Now our gifts to each other, to friends, neighbours, and relatives, parallel the supreme gift to the world, Christ Himself. His coming, as the Messiah, was foretold; and it is worth our while to go back to the prophecy in Isaiah (9: 6-7; 11: 2).

Some of you may have heard the term "self-fulfilling prophecy", one which needs no gift of foresight, but which comes about simply because we say it will happen: I tell someone that he is a fool, and lo and behold, he behaves like a fool. Jesus was accused by the cynics of His age of being a mere charlatan taking advantage of Isaiah's prophecy, and making it come true for His own ends. The prophecy was seen by many as merely voicing men's deep desire for peace and concord, a pious hope rather than a confident prediction. But the whole of the Book of Isaiah, and one passage in particular (chapter 35) is one message of hope and confidence, and not of desperation or ill-founded yearning. One or two could see through the misery we laughingly call the human condition to the certainty that things could, must, would be better; and that a "Messiah", a man truly of God, would come to show us the way. When he arrived, however, there were several, not least his own cousin, John the Baptist, who questioned what he was doing. They perhaps expected someone who would lead the Jews into battle, who would take the political fight to the Romans; instead they met Jesus. He did none of these things. He gave us the clue Himself, drawing attention to the works which He had performed (Matthew 11); in this way He fulfilled the prophecies in a way which was not expected, but which would prove to be far more effective in the long run.

So what else lies behind that first unique Christmas gift? Here I am on very dodgy ground; and I know that many would question my idea. Jesus claimed to be the Son of *Man*; others claimed him as the Son of *God*. I find no contradiction, though Christians have tended to make difficulties where there should be none. Humans have invested Christ with all the qualities of God while at the same time trying to place on him all the limitations of our own frail humanity. From that they have argued that no mere human can aspire to true godliness.

I find this very sad. For me the true message of Christmas is that for the first time a *man* arrived on earth to show us that humans *could* so aspire. The very fact of his being human opened the way to heaven; showed that human frailty could be conquered; freed us from the stifling effects of despair and resignation – *if* we were prepared to follow his example and precepts. It is not easy – far from it. GK Chesterton once said that no-one could claim that Christianity did not work, since it had never been tried properly. Can we try? Can you?

Points to Ponder

What does Christmas mean for you?
Should Christmas have any significance for non-Christians?
If so, what can they read into it?
Why are so many people chary of celebrating Christmas,
instead labelling it "Winterval" or some other meaningless term?

ON COMMITMENT

In these times the very word "commitment" is almost a dirty word – we are afraid of it. Every day we are asked in some measure, in some way or other, to make a commitment. We may wish to join a club, a society, an organisation; we will be asked to show a formal acceptance of the rules of that club, that society and thus we make a commitment. A very senior member of the Scouts once said that there were only two things about Scouting that were voluntary: when one joined, and when one left; and he added that the second was not always so voluntary! In other words, we can remain a member for as long as we are prepared to accept the rules; if we cannot accept the rules, we should leave. It worries me that so many people join an organisation, knowing full well what the rules are, and then take all manner of actions to show that they are not prepared to accept those rules, while still insisting on their right to remain a member. That seems to me to be utter nonsense.

This is the meaning of contracts. When we take up employment most of us have to sign a contract which binds us to behave in a certain way: it may lay down the circumstances in which we can leave – having to give a certain amount of notice, or even paying some compensation if we break the contract. At one time those contracts were sealed by no more than a handshake, which was considered as binding as any other form of commitment, "An Englishman's word is his bond", as we used to be able to say; now everything has to be committed to paper, so that everyone, including the inevitable lawyers, knows what has been agreed. However, even the existence of a contract is considered by many to be no longer binding, especially if the contract becomes too "onerous". But the breaking of a contract, especially unilaterally, is the breaking of a trust; and such ruptures are destructive of what holds our civilisation together.

Unfortunately this is all too true of that most sacred of contracts, marriage. In the old days marriage was a public ceremony: a young man and a young woman made their vows before a large "audience", who were in effect witnesses of a binding contract; and their help was expected to ensure that the contract remained binding. Perhaps, too, the seriousness of the vows was underlined by that public affirmation. Now, like so many other affirmations, such "vows" are taken more discreetly; they are therefore not taken so seriously; and can be broken at will, whatever the "collateral damage" which might arise, among children, relatives, even friends.

All relationships, whether they are those between an employer and an employee, or between business partners, or between a husband and wife, go through sticky patches. Many people recognise this and know that the relationship has to be worked at to be maintained, and even more so if it is considered to be intrinsically worthwhile. What is so sad is that too many people are not prepared to make that effort; and we are perhaps only now coming to realise the corrosive effects of that lack of commitment.

Those who support a football team, or a pop star, already know about commitment. They go on supporting even when the odds are stacked against "my" team or "my" favourite: "for better or worse"; they go on lending support even when fortunes seem to be slipping: "for richer or poorer"; they go on backing those chosen heroes from the team or the pop group even when they rather let the side down: "in sickness or in health". If support – commitment – can be given to a mere football team, or a mere pop idol, can it be given to an employer, a wife or husband, a family? And if not – why not?

Points to Ponder

Should we accept that one can dishonour a promise – as has already happened – simply because it "was only a verbal agreement"?
Is it unreasonable to expect people to honour promises made, even if their fulfilment becomes difficult or inconvenient?
Is there any point to such a level of "trustworthiness"?

ON CONSCIENCE

A hundred or so years ago a man by the name of Sigmund Freud was practising as a doctor in Vienna. His experiences led him to consider the mental aspects of illness – so much so that he became known as the father of modern psychology. Most of his thinking has now been developed beyond recognition; indeed some of his ideas have long since been dismissed as quite unreasonable. But one feature was his rather arbitrary division of the personality into three layers. The first of these was the *ego*, really only the Latin word for "me": this was the public face which we all present to the world. Beneath this was the *id* – again the Latin word for "it". This embraced the primitive person, with all his uncontrolled lusts and passions. But above was the *superego*, which tried to control our *id* – if you like, our conscience. The true ego was therefore the personality which emerged from the conflicts between the *id* and the *superego*.

Freud went on to propose that the *superego* was an integral and natural part of our personality, that we were born with it, and that we all benefited from the presence of a force which would inhibit our wilder passions. He suggested that, since animals seemed to be able to resist mutual self-destruction, so man ought also to be able to do so. He noticed that man was just about the only species whose members were capable of killing each other. Now we seem to have to accept that this so-called conscience has to be learned, like so much else of what makes us truly human.

Some time ago there was a rather nasty murder in Milton Keynes. Four young thugs set about a boy of seventeen. This boy was short-sighted; so they took his glasses and smashed them, before mugging him in the most violent fashion. The boy could not swim, either; so they took him to a bridge over a fast-running and deep river, and dropped him in. His body was later fished out several miles away. After the case was brought to court, and the attackers convicted, an article appeared in the *Spectator*, whose author tried – and failed – to find any reasonable grounds for this thuggish behaviour. He worried that there seemed to be no acceptable reason for such actions on the part of the four young men. But letters in the magazine's correspondence columns showed greater concern that they had no reason *not* to behave as they did: in other words Freud's inhibitors were simply not there. Evidence, perhaps, that society needs to teach the underlying precepts of decent behaviour: the way in which we treat each other, in such a way as to make life for all more bearable, more civilised. Even now we have the spectacle of youngsters picking on the weak and defenceless – and filming themselves on video or digital camera, catching themselves "in the act". How macabre is that?

In a school or any other institution rules are a means of putting such an ethical framework into place. The underlying principle should be that of consideration for and courtesy towards others; all the rules have that as their aim – the protection of the weaker against the stronger, the inhibition of insensitive actions against others. Charles Kingsley made the point with one of his characters, Mrs Do-as-you-would-be-done-by: we should act towards others as we would wish them to behave towards us. There is a much older code still, based on the same principles – the Ten Commandments; and later Jesus' own two: Love God, love your neighbour. Our own code should always be asking the question: How would I feel to be on the receiving end of this action? If the answer is, not very happy – then don't do it!

Points to Ponder

Why are we seemingly no longer able to inculcate a sense of responsibility to the "other person"?
How do we make people aware of the consequences of their actions?
Is it possible, or indeed even reasonable, to try to do so?
What has happened to shame?

ON DEATH

I thank God that in school we were very seldom brought face to face with the reality of death. In the normal course of events we do not expect school friends to die, or even for teachers to leave us so suddenly in this way. Statistics bear this out: the vast majority of us will fulfil at least the Biblical life-span of three score years and ten, with many of us nowadays expecting to top the full century. Despite the gloom and doom of the newspapers and TV, we live in an increasingly healthy world, where all the more common ailments, and many of the less common ones, are bit by bit being conquered by better hygiene and better treatment.

But death is still there. It is the one inescapable fact of life. Several times in my professional life I had to attend the funerals of colleagues who have been called before their time, either as the result of accidents or after illness. Often, even in the midst of sadness at the loss of a friend, one can feel a small sense of relief that death has prevented any further suffering, when cancer or some other debilitating disease has been the cause of death. As we get older we face our demise with increasing equanimity – we get used to the idea that we are not immortal, and hopefully we can at least in some part look back on a life which has been well-spent and useful. For those of us with some religious faith the thought of an after-life is some comfort: most people I know who profess a faith do not fear death or what lies afterwards, even though they might fear the dying.

But the shock of losing a friend or colleague can be traumatic. Again during my professional life I had to witness the loss of pupils: one to a quite horrible road accident outside the school gates; another to being knocked off his bicycle; at least three to illness; and one quite terrible case of suicide. The gaps left by such deaths as these can be very hard to get used to or to understand; and there will always be the temptation to rail against a God who can let such things happen. But that is the one thing we should not do: for often the causes of such events are down to us; our own carelessness or thoughtlessness might be at the bottom of such accidents; or we might not yet have discovered a remedy for a hitherto incurable disease. That loss should instead act as the spur to be more watchful, or to work to discover new remedies.

Lastly, for many, death is a doorway into a new phase of life. Many older people claim to talk to their dead spouses, to share experiences or to ask for advice. Joyce Grenfell, before she died, quoted this poem:

If I should go before the rest of you,
Break not a flower nor inscribe a stone,
Nor when I'm gone speak in a Sunday voice,
But be the usual selves that I have known.
Weep if you must,
Parting is hell;
But life goes on,
So sing as well.

There are also these words of comfort, written by Henry Scott Holland which are often quoted at funerals:

"Death is nothing at all – I have only slipped away into the next room. Whatever we were to each other, that we are still. Call me by my old familiar name, speak to me in the easy way which you always used. Laugh as we always laughed at the little jokes we enjoyed together. Play, smile, think of me, pray for me. Let my name be the household word that it always was; let it be spoken without effort. Life means all that it ever meant. It is the same as it ever was; there is absolutely unbroken continuity. Why should I be out of your mind because I am out of your sight? I am but waiting for you, for an interval, somewhere very near just around the corner. All is well. Nothing is past; nothing is lost. One brief moment and all will be as it was before – only better, infinitely happier; and for ever we will all be one together with Christ."

Points to Ponder

Have you experienced the death of a loved one, a friend, a neighbour or a family member?
How do you react to the news of death?
Most subjects once taboo are now no longer. Why can we not talk about death in the same easy way?

ON DISCIPLESHIP

In the Old Testament we read the story of Samuel. As a boy Samuel was offered to the Temple by his mother Hannah, and he lived and worked there under the priest Eli. If we believe the book, Eli was a wicked and neglectful priest, and his sons were quite evil young men. Perhaps in our more tolerant days we would see Eli as a weak and ineffectual father – but no more. Perhaps he was tired, of his work, of his family, even perhaps of life. Samuel's arrival gave him back his interest; and even more so when the boy had his dream and thought that Eli was calling him in the middle of the night. Twice Eli sent the boy back to his bed; and on the third occasion he recognised that God was calling Samuel, and told him how to respond.

You may have seen or heard this: "He that knows not, and knows not that he knows not – shun him, for he is a fool; he that knows not, and knows that he knows not – teach him, for he will learn; he that knows, and knows not that he knows – wake him, for he is asleep; he that knows, and knows that he knows – follow him, for he is wise". Children come into this secondary school at the age of eleven; they are for the most part in that first group – the know-nothings. But teachers cannot shun them, least of all because none of them are such fools, but also certainly because it is the duty of a teachers to do something about that unknowing. In the course of a few years the aim is to turn them into members at least of that second group, if not the last. The first task is to awaken them to the possibilities before them, to show what is there to be learned, or experienced, or shared. Then to demonstrate just how far there is yet to travel and to make them face up to the realities of their ignorance. The need thereafter is to inspire them to do something about the vast gaps in their knowledge and experience, and to go out and explore, and become one of those who know that they don't know.

It is not just the recognition of ignorance that is important, but the willingness and the ability to do something about it. Aristotle was among the first to remark that we are given two ears, but only one mouth; and that it is therefore sensible to listen twice as much as we speak. Someone, more recently, pointed out that when we speak we merely repeat what we already know; when we listen we might just learn something new. That is what discipleship is about. That word along, oddly, with the word discipline, comes from the Latin word meaning to learn. Samuel learned how to listen, in the dark recesses of the Temple, and Eli taught him how to learn from his experience. Samuel went on to become one of the major figures in Old Testament history, and later consecrated Saul as the new King of the Hebrew people. Christ had his disciples those to whom he chose to teach his message, and then to go forth and pass it on to the world. Everyone needs to learn to listen and, even more importantly, to learn from what is heard, to interpret what is learned and then to put into practice what is interpreted. As Christ reminded us, he who has ears to hear, let him hear.

Points to Ponder

How can teachers or leaders, convey a love of learning to their pupils and followers?

How do they inculcate an "amor sciendi" – the love of knowledge for its own sake?

ON DISCIPLINE

D iscipline is – especially for young people – a desperately fraught subject. There are so many contradictions: the need to be free and independent, and yet the insistence on obedience to a code which they had no part in framing; and which seems banal and trivial in the extreme. Teenagers are at the most stressful and uncertain period of their lives. They want to be treated as adults – when it suits them; but they want also to enjoy the privilege of reverting to childhood – when it suits them. But whether at any given time they are a "child" or an "adult", they still need a code of conduct – a background of discipline – to see them through. Ultimately the only sort of discipline which counts is the control which is exerted over oneself. It is not easy to learn on one's own when self-control is necessary, or even what sort of self-control is necessary, unless we are shown by example.

There is another side to the question. Several years ago I heard of a school in South London where discipline had all but broken down. The teachers of one department decided that, come what may, they needed good order in their lessons if any good work was to be done. Against the odds, they did at least in part succeed. What rather surprised them was the number of children who came to them, rather than to their more "liberal" colleagues, when they had problems to be solved or questions to be answered. That is something that teachers and leaders need to realise: everyone despite what they may say or even believe, responds better to a sense of order and purpose than to a situation where chaos and mayhem reign.

We hear a great deal these days about human rights; and we have perhaps yet to go through the painful business of sorting out the rights and wrongs of cases where the human rights of two aggrieved parties are seen to clash. There are no rights without responsibilities, no privileges without duties; and the sooner that we recognise the need to respect the rights of others, all others, the better life will become. Put more simply, I cannot do as I wish; whatever I may feel, doing something which needlessly offends or hurts someone else is wrong. The argument must never be that of so many people: "Can I get away with it?" but "Am I hurting anyone by acting in this way?" Someone once said that most people live on the cafeteria principle – self-service only. That way lies anarchy.

Many of us will sooner or later gain some position of authority over other people. We have to learn the subtle distinction between being authoritative: knowing what we are doing; and being authoritarian: being bossy for its own sake. We should bear in mind that no-one ever succeeded in leading unless first having learned how to follow. Too many people expect others to follow orders blindly; too many try to persuade others to question orders as a matter of course. Very seldom is wise guidance received on how to recognise when authority should be accepted. That guidance is what teachers and leaders should be striving to give to others.

Points to Ponder

Why do young people especially find it difficult to accept the authority of others?

Can schools be more effective in teaching the virtues of self-discipline? How could they do so?

ON DUTY

O ne of the Church of England collects enjoins us to think much of our duties and little of our rights. What an unfashionable idea that is today! Yet it is so very true that we can enjoy no rights without taking on board the parallel duties, no privileges without the parallel responsibilities. Someone asked recently why there was no European Commission for Human Responsibilities, to parallel that for Human Rights; a good point. One person's rights are after all another's responsibilities – and vice versa. Someone once quipped that in the old Tsarist Russia people exploited each other; in the Soviet Union it was the other way round.

We in fact owe each other a duty of care, which has little or nothing to do with our rights as human beings. That comes from our living together in tribes, herds, clans or whatever: we have to be prepared to accept the duty to look out for each other if we are to live peacefully and in harmony with each other. Christ summed it up in his second commandment, that we should love our neighbour; and even told us that no-one could claim to love God if he did not also love his brother or his neighbour. When questioned by a man who wanted to know who his neighbour was, Christ told one of his parables, the story of the Good Samaritan. You will know the story, of a man who "fell among thieves" on his way from Jerusalem, and was left to die on the road. Three men came that way: the first, a priest, we are told went by on the other side; as did a Levite – a Temple assistant. But the third was a Samaritan, who did all he could to help the injured man, binding his wounds and taking him to an inn for safe keeping. The inner significance of the story has largely been lost to later generations: for the Samaritans were regarded by the Jews of the time as an inferior race, worthless and of no account. Jesus chose this image deliberately, to illustrate his idea that compassion, care, duty to others, must not be limited to those of whom we approve, but is a universal truth overriding national and racial barriers. Hence, too, his commandment to love our enemies.

We still call people who look out for others in this way Samaritans; and there is also an organisation called "The Samaritans", of which you might have heard, and which exists as a port of call for people who are depressed, desperate or even suicidal – they need only to phone up and they can talk to a helper who is a good listener. And indeed anyone who answers the call from those needing help or support is doing his duty to his fellow human being.

But that is not the end of the story. Throughout life things are expected of us. In school there are duties owed, to teachers, to friends, perhaps even to the idea of the school, its ethos, as it is known. This idea of duty, of obligation goes on, for as life progresses there are further duties, to work mates, to employers, even to the firm's "ethos". And even more duties and obligations, to family, your sons and daughters, possibly even to ageing parents. Society, our clan or tribe or herd, demands that we fulfil those duties. However, banging on for ever about our rights, to the exclusion of all else, can mean but one thing, that those who owe us a duty will feel that they need no longer do so. Our herd, or tribe, or clan, will then simply collapse for there will be no "social cohesion" to hold it together. And all for the want of what is known as "give and take".

Points to Ponder

Can we enjoy rights without accepting the concomitant responsibilities?
Should we not concentrate less on the rights of a given group,
who may seem to be in some way disadvantaged, such as animals,
the elderly or children, and more on the duty of care that we all
owe members of those groups?

ON EASTER

Some time ago I re-read a book, one of the first to suggest that Stonehenge was rather more than just a random collection of old stones, and that it was in fact an ancient and highly elegant computer. The author of this book set out to demonstrate that one could use it to predict eclipses of the sun and moon; and more importantly to set the seasons of the year, along with its more notorious ability to fix the date of Midsummer's Day. From this we can deduce what most sensible people might have guessed – that the seasons were important to our primitive ancestors. Indeed for people dependent on the weather and the seasons to a far greater extent than we are, spring, harvest and the turn of the year were of paramount importance. Festivals at these times were also therefore very important, and were marked by all manner of rituals which to our more sophisticated understanding were no more than superstitious mumbo-jumbo. Nevertheless there was an underlying significance which we would do well to bear in mind. It was no coincidence that the early Christians attached their own celebrations to these older and well-established ceremonials. Easter was just such a season, for the rebirth of the year was important if crops were to bear fruit later in the year.

At Eastertide we all feel a new life stirring: the weather turns just a little milder; the trees and bushes are putting out their new green; the first flowers are showing in our gardens and woodlands and hedgerows. There is the promise of better things to come, as we put the long winter behind us, and we welcome the strengthening sun of summer. For uniformed organisations the Easter weekend often marks the opening of the camping season. At the same time, and most appropriately, all Christians celebrate the most important and the most joyful festival of the Church's calendar, the risen Christ. Cynics will insist that the miracle of the Resurrection simply could not, and therefore did not, happen; for true Christians it is a matter of faith and for them scientific explanations are quite immaterial. What is true is the reality of rebirth, new life from the dead, just as the seed has to die before the new plant can emerge; all this behind the often obscure symbolism. As Jesus rose from the dead at Easter, so can we look forward to the new life promised us.

I remember a "reverend" friend of mine telling a story about butterflies and bullfrogs. Both these creatures, beautiful in their own way, emerged from a previous "life" which was nothing like their new state: one from a chrysalis, the other from a tadpole. Our own lives can mirror this transformation, as our old inadequate poor selves die, leaving a new and we hope "better" person in their place. Can we rise, not only to the promise of Easter, but also to its challenge?

Points to Ponder

Does Easter have any significance for you?
Apart from the religious aspects, do you see Easter as a time of renewal?
Can you accept the story of the Resurrection?

ON ELECTIONS

Every so often we are able to enjoy all the delights of a General Election. I am particularly interested in the ways in which politicians abuse language. As a former language teacher I am concerned about the thoughts we have, and the words we choose to express those thoughts. I am also concerned about the ways in which language can be distorted, to say things which are not intended, or to hide the speaker's true intentions. I have often tried to spell out the importance of listening to what the politicians are saying, and to try to establish what they mean as opposed to what they say. Not as easy as it might sound: for discrimination, the art of distinguishing between the true and the bogus, is one of our most difficult tasks. We have to learn to think for ourselves, to make value judgements which are valid, to criticise in a positive and constructive fashion.

Governments in particular, but also all political parties, are adept at promising the earth. We have been encouraged by them in our faith in the omnipotence of governments. Politicians are fond of having us believe that they, and the governments they support, can do anything – and moreover that they should do everything. However one needs only to look at the historical record to see that this is not so. True, there are some tasks which only governments, using the powers which we, the electors, are prepared to grant them, can carry out. But the only regimes which can in fact come close to fulfilling this promise are the totalitarian ones; and even they will fail if they work against, rather than with nature, human or botanical. The worst excesses of Stalinism or Fascism are but one example of that sort of over-control.

There are other ways in which this belief can do us harm. Because the Government will "deal with" poverty, or sickness, or homelessness, we do not need to take thought for these problems and there is a death of the charitableness which should be in all of us. Further, we do not need to take thought for ourselves, whether we fall ill, or lose our homes, or go bankrupt: the Government will exercise its "responsibility" on our behalf. If we are now less compassionate, less charitable, less understanding than we used to be, it is as much to do with this loss, this perhaps not altogether unconscious surrender, of personal responsibility as it is with any overt actions on the part of government, of whatever political colour.

If we look again at the historical record, we will see that all "welfare" developments have been nothing to do with governments. The first schools, universities, hospitals and poor-houses were established by the churches. Colonialism was based not on governmental empire-building but on the work of missionaries who were concerned to spread their message. The slave trade was ended, improvements in our care of the sick and poverty-stricken, in sanitation or medical treatments, were brought about, not by government action but by the efforts, often very lonely, of concerned individuals. So what should be our own attitude? We should try to see through the "bread and circuses" approach of too many who would be our governors; and instead recall the words of President John F Kennedy: "Ask not what your country can do for you, rather what you can do for your country". But it was all said a great deal earlier, by St Matthew (25: 34-46).

Points to Ponder

Does voting still have a significance?
When the time comes, will you cast your vote?
Or will you abstain, saying that you cannot influence what happens?
Would it be a good or a bad thing to make voting compulsory?

ON EVIL

One of the most common questions asked of those with a faith in God is why God – any God – can allow the evil which is so obvious in our world. If there were truly a beneficent God, one who believed in making a perfect world, he could not possibly allow the evil things which happen so frequently to happen, or would at least give us the strength to do something about them.

The first thing to remember is that God gave us free will, that is the ability to choose our actions, whether good or evil. What is often forgotten is the old proverb, adopted in some form by many different cultures and societies: "Take what you want; and pay for it." What this means is that we must learn to live with the consequences of our actions. A man called Herbert Spencer, who lived in the time of Queen Victoria, said: "The only result of shielding people from the consequences of their own folly is to fill the world with fools". In other words a great deal of the pain which we suffer as human beings is our own fault; and it is no bad thing to be made to face up to those consequences. Religion makes play with the idea that we are punished for our sins; some people think that we are more punished *by* our sins. That is perhaps no bad thing: provided that we can take on board the lessons that are there to be learned.

The next thing to remember is that we are mortal – we are going to die, sometime, somehow. Most people die of simple old age, they wear out. If it were not so, the world would become a remarkably crowded place. A lot more die of disease or illness; God *has* given us the strength to do something about that: we have doctors, nurses, researchers, all trying to alleviate that sort of pain and suffering. Quite a few people die as the result of accidents, or violence, or wars; and that is something which we alone as human beings can cure. For accidents, or violence, or wars, are the result of man exercising his right to free will, but in an evil way; it is *not* God's responsibility, except in so far as he granted us that free will.

The last thing to remember is that we live in a world fraught with danger. The world itself is a "living organism": it suffers droughts and floods, earthquakes and tidal waves, storms and gales. We can learn from experience what parts of the world are more dangerous than others and then avoid them, or at least take precautions to lessen the dangers. Recently many people have suffered quite disastrous floods; but if, like the man in the Bible who built his house upon the sands, we choose to build our houses on a river's flood plain, we must expect to be flooded. That too is down to man. We are back to the Greek concept of *hubris*, over-weening pride, and *nemesis*, the revenge of the Gods. If we tempt fate, fate will find some way of punishing us. If we wish to avoid evil, for the great part the remedies lie in our own hands.

Some ancient thinkers believed that God had planted all these difficulties with the one purpose of giving us the opportunity to glorify him by our efforts to overcome them. That idea is perhaps a little far-fetched these days; but can we – can you – go out, today and in the future, with the intention of doing *your* little bit to overcome them?

Points to Ponder

Is evil – true evil – always man-made?

How much of what we think wrong with our world can we cure by our own efforts?

What do you think about the idea of free will? Can we take refuge in the idea of not being masters of our own fate – or is that a lazy cop-out?

ON FORGIVENESS

I n the Lord's Prayer we find the words: "Forgive us our trespasses, as we forgive those who trespass against us". One of the questions put to Jesus was about the extent of our forgiveness. His answer was seventy times seven – in other words, we should go on forgiving. Why?

Many years ago I read an article by a psychologist who explained the quite sound psychological reasoning behind a great deal of what the Bible has to say about human relations. He made the point that self-love, or self-esteem, is an essential part of our makeup. He referred his patients suffering from guilt complexes and the like to the story of the Prodigal Son who, having reached a state of shocked realisation of what he had done and become, enjoyed the unconditional forgiveness of his father, and indeed, what is sometimes overlooked, that his father ran to meet him, more than half way. What is done cannot be undone; but if we are prepared humbly to acknowledge our wrong we are safe in the knowledge of having had the slate wiped clean. Freud went rather further: he suggested that where forgiveness was not forthcoming the patient tended to repress the original sin and let it slip out of the conscious mind; and that led to even more problems of a psychological nature. We need in effect to know that we are forgiven if our self-esteem is to be restored. This is the basis of Catholic ideas about confession. I know that confession and absolution can be, and are, badly abused; but the basic idea is sound, that people will find it easier to make a fresh start, "turn over a new leaf", if they start with a clean sheet.

We have therefore a right to expect forgiveness for our misdeeds. I do not altogether agree that forgiveness should be granted willy-nilly; if the sinner is not really prepared to ask for forgiveness, he cannot be ready to take the first step towards redemption – the acknowledgement of fault. Once that first step has been taken, the "sinner" is ready to try to make amends, and might also be ready to accept help in his efforts; as did the Prodigal Son. We may have the right to forgiveness; but all rights have attendant obligations: Jesus so often gave God's forgiveness and blessing, but he always gave the injunction: "Go and sin no more!"; He knew that, once the slate had been wiped clean, we all need to feel encouraged to do better in future. We need to follow Jesus' example of hating the sin but loving the sinner; we need to ask whether forgiveness is to be a spur to fresh efforts, or merely a safety net for the incorrigible.

It is all of course a tall order, to ask for forgiveness. Perhaps it is asking even more, that we should be ready to forgive others. As human beings we cannot always command the proverbial patience of saints. Many of us have experienced others' unwillingness always to forgive; and I know that sometimes forgiveness is regarded as a sign of either weakness or approval in the face of wrong. I have found that however, after some unpleasantness, bringing the protagonists face to face and making each of them ask the other's forgiveness, actually works. I cannot help feeling that the plea in the Lord's Prayer might perhaps be better thus: "May we forgive our debtors, and they us, as we know you forgive our debts to you". I should remind you of the man who, seeing a condemned man on his way to the gallows, said: "There but for the grace of God go I." We none of us get what we truly deserve and for that we should give deep and heartfelt thanks.

Points to Ponder

Do you find it easy to ask for forgiveness?
How difficult is it to admit your faults?
How would you respond if someone who had hurt you in some way were to ask your forgiveness? Negatively; or positively?

ON FREEDOM

W hat is freedom? What do we mean by the word? Most people might claim with some justification that it means simply the right to act as one pleases, with no regard for others. But that is too selfish, too narrow an interpretation. We need perhaps to tackle it from two very different perspectives.

The first might be considered as freedom **from**: the United Nations laid down certain freedoms – freedom from want, from fear, from hunger. In other words we need to be able to conduct our lives without having constantly to worry about the sheer basic necessities of life. Many of our charities began their existence with that in mind: to alleviate those things which made life at best uncomfortable, at worst quite intolerable. Today all the relief agencies, whether charitable or government-led, try to do the same for people in those regions of the globe which do not enjoy the same "freedoms" as ourselves. There is the underlying belief that people cannot be in any real sense "free" if they have to live under the shadow of poverty, hunger or terror. In Great Britain we enjoy a measure of freedom in this first sense, which is well beyond the comprehension of many of those in Africa or Asia or even South America; we have therefore a duty to try to bring those freedoms to those who still lack them.

The second might be considered as freedom **for:** freedom to do certain things; and again certain such freedoms are now taken as read – freedom of speech, of religion, of association. Again, there are many regions of the world which do not enjoy such freedoms, or perhaps even where they are forbidden. We still have that duty to try to allow people in such places to exercise the freedoms which we all too often take for granted, even when they are as at present under severe attack. There are many who will disagree, but it is arguable that all the wars of the past couple of hundred years have been at least in part in defence of the freedoms which we are pleased to enjoy. John Philpot Curran, an Irish lawyer and politician in the eighteenth and early nineteenth centuries, gave us his view that "The condition upon which God hath given liberty to man is eternal vigilance; which condition if he break, servitude is at once the consequence of his crime, and the punishment of his guilt."

Lord Acton, in one of his now-famous dictums, noted that governments do not always possess the freedom to do what they feel is necessary: they have often to give way to *force majeure* – restrictions imposed by other more powerful bodies, considerations of fairness or of other laws, whatever. In his play *Maria Stuart,* Schiller has Queen Elizabeth I talk of the freedom to do what needs to be done, when she is told that Mary is guilty of treason. In the same play Mary finds that in fact she has been granted complete freedom, not, surprisingly, through any direct action to free her by her persecutors, but because she has been deprived of everything; which leaves her free to do and say just what she wishes. We may not be so free: like those politicians, we may find that our freedom to act as we wish is heavily limited.

And rightly, too. We need to strike a delicate balance between our own desire to exercise freedom and that of our neighbours to do likewise. We need to realise that there is really no such thing on earth as untrammelled freedom; that we must not so abuse our own rights that others' rights are similarly abused; that we need to take others into account before we claim the right to act as we wish. As someone once remarked, when liberty destroys order, the hunger for order will destroy liberty, and we seem in our present-day society to be very near that point. But there is also a German saying: "Freiheit ist eigentlich nicht anders als die Fähigkeit, mit den Folgen der eigenen Entscheidungen zu leben." – Freedom is really no more than the ability to live with the consequences of one's own decisions. Lastly there is the paradoxical but very real belief, in one of our prayers, that we will find perfect freedom in the service of Our Lord.

Points to Ponder

Can we really exercise proper freedom without some sense of responsibility?

To what extent do we as a society have the right to interfere with individual freedom?

ON GOOD AND EVIL

When I was at school one of the plays we performed was *Mr Bolfry*, by James Bridie. In the play Mr Bolfry personifies the Devil. In one scene he says that he is quite essential in the scheme of things, for without evil there can be no good, without night there can be no day, without black there can be no white. Instinctively, I suppose, we know that he is right; and, at least for most of us, the difference between the two is often clear. Most of us also know that to do the right is always better in the long run than to do the wrong, whatever the immediate attractions; and however often we may in fact fail to do the right thing. There is an old German proverb which tells us that to choose between good and evil is easy; what is hard is to choose the lesser of two evils.

God in his wisdom gave us the freedom to choose – free will. Some people will try to tell you that there is no such thing as free will, for we are all pre-determined, pre-conditioned to behave in a certain way. From the psychologist's point of view there is probably no way of telling one way or the other; but I do believe in free will, just as I also believe in the way in which the consequences of our exercising our free will come back to haunt us. Mark Twain, always there with a pithy word, advised us always to do what is right; in that way we will gratify the few and astonish everyone else. There is also an old proverb, claimed by many different peoples: "Take what you want – and pay for it!"; or in other words, make your choices and learn to live with them. And to exercise free will is to display virtue: for there would be no virtue in being good if there were no alternative; and one could not be condemned for doing evil if one could do no other. That last point is worth looking at in view of what is happening in courts today, where criminals are trying to use their apparent lack of free will as an excuse for their behaviour. Surely if they are still a danger to the public, they should still be locked away.

In schools there is an attempt to set a firm framework for behaviour – what is called the school's ethos. This is true of many other establishments. In this day and age, when any curbs on behaviour are regarded as an infringement of inalienable human rights, to try to set such a code of conduct might be extremely difficult. Nevertheless it must be done: there is a need to show what is felt to be a useful way of living alongside other people and vice versa. No-one should deprive another of the right to choose; but conversely there is a right to try to influence others to follow the right road. The wish to give that guidance is thousands of years old: in Deuteronomy (30: 19-20) Moses told his people: "I call heaven and earth to witness against you today, that I have set before you life and death, blessings and curses. Choose life, that you and your descendants may live, loving the Lord your God, obeying him, and holding fast to Him; for that means life to you and length of days, so that you may live in the land that the Lord swore to give to your ancestors, to Abraham, to Isaac and to Jacob".

Moses gave his followers the right to choose, but tried to influence them to choose wisely. How would you choose?

Points to Ponder

Do you agree that the freedom to choose is the basis of our humanity? To what extent have teachers and leaders the right to try to influence your choices?
How do we teach others to distinguish right from wrong?

ON GRATITUDE

M any things which happen in our society occur not because they should, but because there are men and women about who want to see them happen. In school life this refers to all those activities which help to make a school more of a living community than a simple academic sweat-shop: the games clubs, the hobby societies, the school trips and so on. One of the glories of some schools is the summer activities week, when the school timetable is suspended, and all pupils can take advantage of a week of visits and tours. There are also the "educational" visits to other countries, the ski and other tours, work experience visits, pen-friend visits.

But while all these activities are non-academic, they can still be regarded as educational. In my time I have run clubs for tennis and badminton; and I have enjoyed simply chatting to pupils in their rest-periods. I have led many visits both at home and abroad; and I have found that I can "teach" more in an afternoon of informal talk than in a week of formal lessons. I can remember yarning to small groups while sitting in the sun on the steps of the Palace of Versailles; or walking a beach in Normandy; or in a café on the Kurfürstendamm in Berlin; or strolling the hills of New England. It is an opportunity for teachers to see pupils in a different light – the chance to get to know them much more as individuals. On one trip I undertook I was suddenly made very aware that pupils I had taught for several years were in fact almost complete strangers – having seen them solely as students of French or German, I had no inkling of their aspirations or real talents. In the same way they were able to see a different side of the staff; and there was always the hope that this might make us seem like a human being too!

However, none of these things, indeed nothing that happens anywhere in a school, or any other place, is an end in itself. Those who arrange such events look beyond the everyday in ways that perhaps the participants cannot. Since they cannot see clearly, they then suffer often from the temptation to take things for granted – a tendency to assume that all such activities are a right rather than a privilege. These things are not a right, and those who benefit from them could help to avoid the impression that is sometimes given, by showing due appreciation. I refer to gratitude –

though that term requires closer definition. It is always most gratifying for the leaders when someone comes to you at the end of a successful trip to say "Thank you"; and I cherish the moment when one boy came to me at the end of his school time to tell me that he had enjoyed every one of his outings with me, and that he was immensely grateful for my "having made things happen", which he would not otherwise have been able to enjoy. Likewise it is saddening when pupils cannot respond in this way; worse when their parents are similarly ungracious – I remember returning from Normandy late one dank July night; and not one parent came to acknowledge that his child had had a good time.

Gratitude is not simply a question of saying "Thank you". Many people give an example of selflessness. Gratitude should be, not a matter of doing favours for those who have done you favours, returning a service paid, or even merely being grateful; but of following that example, of going out and doing likewise, of giving of ourselves for the service of others in our circle.

Points to Ponder

Which activities have you really enjoyed?
Have you ever said "Thank you" to those involved in the organisation?
Do you feel inspired to "go and do likewise"?
Do you have any talent for organisation?
Or any talent which you might put at the disposal of others?

ON HARVEST TIME

At the Harvest Festival in my Church we sang a modern hymn

God in His love for us lent this planet,
gave it a purpose in time and in space,
small as a spark from the fire of creation,
cradle of life and the home of our race.

(Rejoice & Sing 85)

Many years ago the idea of stewardship came into fashion: the idea that all the good things that we enjoy on this earth were ours to hold in trust, to use as we needed, but not so to despoil that future generations could not use them in their turn. The concept applied not only to material goods, but also to money, to time, to energy and imagination – all gifts which we count as truly human. This was conservation at its noblest: not to waste, not so to use that no one else could use, not so to abuse that the use was destroyed. The theory at least was that science would enable us to make a better use of our resources, and to ensure that no-one, anywhere, would want for food and water, shelter or good health.

Whilst many people still hold this attitude, there is always a stronger force at work: sheer unadulterated greed. The short-sightedness of politicians, of businessmen, of industrialists has seen the destruction of this planet's reserves in a quite terrible fashion; and that damage may quite possibly prove to be irreversible. That damage is not just the direct result of slash-and-burn policies in South America or, recently and spectacularly, in the Pacific Basin; but also the indirect result of war, as in the Middle East, in Iraq; or of carelessness, as with the huge oil-spill at Valdez, in Alaska; or of over-use, as with the deforestation of vast areas of Northern India; or of misguided agricultural policies, as has happened within the European Community. To quote that hymn again:

Long have our human wars ruined its harvest,
long has earth bowed to the terror of force;
long have we wasted what others have need of,
poisoned the fountain of life at its source.

We cannot claim ignorance on these matters. Our newspapers, our radios, our television sets, all are constantly bringing to our attention the results of our folly, and spelling out for us their causes. It cannot always be "the other person's responsibility"; we can all do our little bit to reduce the rampant damage being wrought by our consumerist society; the destruction caused by irresponsible and unaccountable politicians and businessmen. Simply tinkering at the edges – like a recent irrelevant proposal to put all developing countries on the Internet, when their peoples have no electricity, but need food and water – will solve nothing. It may mean a rather lower standard of living for the few; a small price to pay if the result is a higher standard of living – or even a matter of pure survival – for the many. The last verse of that hymn might well serve as a final prayer:

Earth is the Lord's: it is ours to enjoy it,
ours, as His stewards, to farm and defend.
From its pollution, misuse and destruction,
good Lord, deliver us, world without end!
Amen

Points to Ponder

How do we ensure a fairer distribution of the earth's richness?
Jesus told us that the poor will always be with us.
How do we try to alleviate the suffering which that poverty brings?
Most charities do a marvellous job in helping those in need.
How do we ensure that they spend our money wisely?

ON HEROES

" Happy the land that has no need of heroes" so said Bertolt Brecht – he was talking about the unhappy land of Germany under Hitler, and the need for heroes to resist that evil. In other circumstances it is perhaps one of the more meaningless reflections, for we all have a need of heroes those people who deserve our respect, admiration, emulation. We all need a model on whom to shape our own behaviour, our own actions, our own way of life.

Of late we have become suspicious of heroes. Those whom we have been brought up to respect often suffer attacks on their reputations, usually after they die, and are no longer able to defend themselves. It's almost as if we cannot abide the presence of such paragons of virtue against whom we must be measured and compared. We judge others not by the standards of their own age, but against our own norms, more "valid", more "relevant", but sadly all too often more debased, more perverted. Churchill, who sixty years ago almost single-handedly led the struggle to maintain the freedoms we take for granted, is not to be respected because "he was a drunkard". Montgomery, who led our forces during WW2 with such distinction, is not to be respected because "he might have been gay". Countless politicians of distinction have similarly been denigrated, often on the grounds that they have said something, often taken violently out of context, which a small clique have found unacceptable. When I was a Scout, a Senior Scout, our patrols were named after heroes – Mallory, Scott, Grenfell, Drake – all of whom have become victims of accusations of political incorrectness. Very sad. Disraeli once said: "Great services are not cancelled by one act or one single error"; but the trouble is that these days they are, and with a vengeance.

Yet we still need heroes. Perhaps not those who might appeal to particular ideas: those pop idols who must command our respect despite being addicted to drugs; those football stars who must command our respect despite being wife-beaters, or thuggish louts, or drunkards; those who would be our national leaders despite being tainted by sleaze or messy affairs or divorces; those religious or moral leaders who demean their position by their arrogance or selfishness. In so many cases Disraeli's sentiment has been upended – one good quality must be seen as redeeming an otherwise quite terrible example. Because we are all human, we are going – all of us – to fall by the wayside in some way or other. Conversely many of us will show, in some way or other, those characteristics which are worthy of respect or admiration. Often they will be unsung heroes: from my own Pantheon, there are; a politician, Ray Gunter, whom no-one now remembers, but who was one of the most upright men ever to reach the House of Commons; a schoolmaster, my own housemaster, whose example to successive generations of schoolboys was outstanding; an old friend, a member of my Church, who quietly served his community in the Citizens' Advice Bureau; another friend from Scouting, who helps deprived children in London's East End; a former Minister of my Church, whose work outside his own "parish" was hardly noticed even by his own congregation and a Catholic priest, a most unassuming man, whose work with those in need is similarly hardly noticed – except by those on the "receiving end".

We should be much readier to overlook, or at the very least forgive, such faults as these people might possess; and instead concentrate on those characteristics which we would do well to copy.

Points to Ponder

Who are your own heroes? Why?
What qualities do you look for in your heroes?
In Ancient Greek mythology, what made a "hero"?

ON IMMORTALITY

One of the central themes of Christianity, and indeed of many other religions, is that of immortality. It is one of the most difficult ideas to grasp, especially in our materialist and scientific society. But it has to be faced, and men and women have grappled with the seeming futility of an existence which seems to end so horribly finally with our death. Different societies have faced it in different ways. The ancient Egyptians so ordered their society that the after-life was all-important; and we still have the evidence of the quite extraordinary rituals which commemorated their passing into a higher existence. The Greeks certainly believed in an after-life, which depended on their performance in this life: humans could aspire to be gods or heroes in the next world, and many of them were so venerated. The Norsemen were very pessimistic in their view of our earthly life, likening it to the short respite which a bird may enjoy when it comes into the warmth and light of a house, seeking refuge from the storm outside. It can enjoy the comfort while it may; but sooner or later it must go out again into the limitless blackness and be lost in oblivion. That image was used by a bishop in the Dark Ages, Paulinus, when he was trying to persuade Edwin, the pagan King of England, to embrace Christianity. In our own time a number of scientists are groping towards the purpose they see in the beautiful order we call nature. The late Fred Hoyle, the famous astronomer and writer, took the uncomfortable view that he really could not tolerate his own company for more than a couple of hundred years. He could not accept the basic Christian premise that our lives and beings are transformed by accepting Christ's message.

I wonder whether the explanation is not, at least in part, a great deal simpler. In psychology we learn about the two instincts: the desire for self-preservation, which leads us to feed and defend ourselves; and the desire for the preservation of the species, which involves our protection of our young and of course the acts of human and animal reproduction. In many ways we as human beings sublimate those drives, and we find different ways of expressing them. So the desire for immortality becomes the driving force behind those of us who wish to leave some trace of our existence here on earth: politicians, leaders, even teachers, who try to influence the lives of others, and to leave behind them the perpetuation of their ideas. Why does an artist paint; why does a writer produce his books, novels or plays; a composer his symphonies and concertos; a sculptor his statues; unless he seeks to leave behind him something by which to be remembered?

We come full circle to the ancient Greeks: two and a half thousand years ago the writer Thucydides wrote: "For the whole earth is the sepulchre of famous men, and their story is not only graven on stone over their native earth, but lives on far away, without visible symbol, woven into the stuff of other men's lives." That is one clue to the meaning of immortality: that what we do here will, in whatever small measure, survive us. Our actions are not perhaps immortal in an individual sense – they become absorbed into what we are pleased to call culture. Christians still believe in the immortality of the soul – that we each as individuals will be welcomed into the cosmos, the all-pervading intelligence we call God. Cynics may scoff: but the Frenchman Blaise Pascal wrote that we should all act as if there is a God. If God does not exist, nothing has been lost; but if he does, everything has been gained. And Ralph Waldo Emerson, the American writer, told us: "Let the soul be assured that somewhere in the universe it should rejoin its friend, and it would be content and cheerful alone for a thousand years".

Points to Ponder

What does "immortality" mean to you?
Would you be comfortable with the idea of living for ever?
How would you wish to be remembered by coming generations?

ON INDIVIDUALISM

Several years ago I read a book, *King of the Castle*; its subtitle was *Choice and Responsibility in the Modern World*. The author, Gai Eaton, writes from considerable experience, as a teacher, journalist, diplomat – and more interestingly, from the point of view of a committed Muslim. He starts with the thesis that we have become detached from the nature of which we are still a part. For this he blames our having lost "religion"; our living and working in ever-larger organisations; and our moving away from our fundamental links with the land.

But why? Here Eaton is at his most negative: for he cites the way in which our century has seen some of the worst cases of man's inhumanity to man, in Hitler's concentration camps, in Stalin's labour camps, and yet we still try to assert that our "civilisation" is an example of the inexorable upward progress of the Western way of life. In reality the sheer size of the organisations in which we live and work, the sheer numbers of people involved in those organisations, are destroying first our individuality and identity and second our sense of responsibility. Modern society needs a docile work force; modern government, interfering as it does in more and more corners of our lives, equally needs an electorate ready to go along with its dictates. Gai Eaton deplores the accretions of legal and other restrictions on our freedom, and especially our freedom to think and to act in accordance with our own consciences. All "free" thinking, all appeals to any higher unworldly authority, are therefore to be discouraged: by ridicule; by censorship; by accusations of insanity; by imprisonment; even in the last resort by execution, liquidation, or "disappearance". At the same time acts which in a more personal context would be condemned as wicked, even evil, can be justified as "for the good of the State", or "for the greater good". Those committing them can take refuge in the Nazi plea "I was only following orders" or in shifting the blame on to a higher ranking functionary. Oddly, this book first appeared in 1977; but how blindingly relevant it seems today!

The world still need individuals, those people who are prepared to stand against the tide. Bertrand Russell, in one of his ten commandments, tells us: "Do not fear to be eccentric in opinion, for every opinion now accepted was once eccentric". Progress is made only by those who are ready to step outside the orthodox, to think the unthinkable – in the words of Thoreau: "If a man does not keep pace with his companions, perhaps it is because he hears a different drummer. Let him step to the music which he hears, however measured and far away". The evidence is all around you: minority views are often better, more valid, than the "received wisdom"; circumstances change, and our opinions *must* change in step.

If education has any true function in society, it must not be to produce lobby fodder, factory fodder, or any other sort of fodder; but individuals prepared to be themselves, and to think for themselves; prepared to look critically at that "received wisdom"; prepared to make thundering nuisances of themselves by drawing attention to proven weaknesses and possible improvements. All attempts to stop that process will lead sooner or later to the nightmares of *1984*, and I have to say that I regard the present tendency to ignore, or even worse to stifle debate, on any great issue facing us, as a long, long step along that route. To quote Bertrand Russell again: "Have no respect for the authority of others, for there are always contrary authorities to be found".

Points to Ponder

Could you stand against the opinions of others, if you thought that you were right and they were wrong?
Consider the lessons of the Resistance Movements during the Second World War. Could you be a member of such a movement?

Books to read:

Gai Eaton – *King of the Castle*
George Orwell – *1984*

ON INDUSTRY

I suppose that the dirtiest four-letter word in any schoolboy's lexicon is "work". Most would far rather be out playing football, or messing about with computers, than sitting in school listening to the teachers. Yet there was once a belief that we were set on earth solely to work; and what became known as the Protestant work ethic was born. Work was held to be a noble thing, ennobling those who worked; while those who did not work were held to be parasites. In the old days this may have been true: work was the sole means of survival, and if you did not work, for yourselves or for others, you were simply a drain on the common good.

We are comparatively wealthy. Even the poorest in our society enjoy a standard of living well beyond that dreamed of by most people over a hundred years ago. We are able to support a growing number of services given by people who do not "produce" in any real material sense, yet whose contribution is in our eyes an essential one. But we now run the danger of the contrast between those who work to live, and those who live to work. Workaholics, those who cannot exist without a constant "fix" of work, are very uncomfortable people to have around, and in many ways cause more heartache than the real skivers. Yet most of us are happier to be active; and even more so to feel that our activity is useful. Many people leading humdrum lives, where their contribution is quite negligible, have found satisfaction in voluntary work, as youth leaders or charity workers or lay preachers or whatever.

All that said, our industrial strength, or rather the lack of it, has come in for a great deal of criticism in the past few years. In the recent past we have seen many of our greatest companies go to the wall: the British car industry is almost defunct; we no longer produce motorcycles or buses; the Westland helicopter scandal several years ago savoured of sheer stupidity; and Sheffield, once the home of the greatest cutlery businesses in the world, now has nothing like that to be proud of. It has become fashionable to blame the power of the trade unions on the one hand, and failings in our educational system on the other, for this decline; and there is a great deal of truth in both ideas.

Recent statistics show that nearly 40% of British school leavers have no relevant qualification when leaving school; in the US the figure is 16%, in Japan 4%. In the average comprehensive school this means that some 70 children each year have nothing to offer to the world of work. In the US that figure would be about 28, in Japan 7. Can we wonder that we are slipping? There are any number of trite explanations: our class system; poor teachers – always that one!; a biased reward system; more poor teachers. This country is not rich in natural resources. Like say Switzerland, we must live by our brains – in which we are very rich: this country has produced more Nobel prize-winners, more useful inventions, comparatively, than any other country. One Oxford college alone has produced more Nobel laureates than France and Germany combined. But we are not good at exploiting those ideas, those talents; and we are quite terrible at rewarding brains and intellectual success – indeed we have a gross talent for decrying and belittling such qualities. It is a tragedy when a school of my acquaintance can boast that "learning is cool": all schools ought to be able to make that boast. Instead, in most cases the mediocre win promotion and huge salaries; they boast that they have succeeded without having to go through all the hard work of study and qualifications. That is the message we have to counter if we are to succeed once more. We need to show that the real innovators, the real risk-takers, are to be cherished as much as those who can exploit their ideas and inventions.

Perhaps even more important, however, is the application we bring to our job. Do we tackle the job with enthusiasm, with a will to succeed, with a sense of service to others, with a desire to do the job as well as we are able? Or do we allow our keenness to wane as we continue to work? Will our firm's customers, those who seek our services, be for ever frustrated because we do not care enough, because we cannot take the trouble to seek out the answers, because we are scared to take the initiative, because we are too complacent?

The Parable of the Talents has a great many messages for us. One of those messages is that we have each and every one of us a number of gifts which we can exploit, for our own benefit as well as for other people's; the servant who hid his talent in the ground was the one who received the severest strictures. What is *your* own attitude? Are you the man who received ten talents, or the fool with his one?

Points to Ponder

How do we as a society instil pride in doing a good job?
What do educationalists need to do to improve matters?
How do we encourage initiative and risk-taking?

ON INITIATIVE

There is an old story, probably apocryphal, about a young soldier who had failed to measure up to a test which he had been set while on exercises. His commanding officer took him aside afterwards to ask him why he did not use his initiative. His reply: "No-one told me to." Rather more seriously, many organisations, and increasingly commercial firms, are expecting their members to take initiative tests, and, more importantly to act on their own initiative when faced with problems. Teachers are left very much to their own devices in the classroom – even in these days when every action is so closely scrutinised from outside; and their effectiveness is often measured by the extent to which they can act on their own "initiative".

Quite often, too, one finds that problems have a habit of solving themselves when and if they are tackled head-on; though in my experience a period of consideration and reflection often helps to tackle the problem in the right way. Sometimes a good deal of imagination might be needed if the problem is to be viewed properly: what became known as lateral thinking, after the work of one Edward De Bono. He showed that training in lateral thinking often led to more satisfactory outcomes than the opposite, linear thinking. We know this from our own experience: you will perhaps have heard that an "unintelligent" linear-thinking computer will tell you that a stopped watch is more reliable than one which runs slow – the stopped watch is right twice a day, the other is never right!

You need also to be prepared to make things happen; that is what is meant by taking the initiative. It means being bold, taking risks, going out on a limb. Taking risks implies that we will sometimes fail; and frankly that does not matter in the slightest; provided that we are prepared to learn from the experience. But every so often we will meet with success – even if we have to accept that it may be only partial, or even not what we might understand by success. People so often will be happy to meet us half way: in my trips to Germany, for example, I have noticed that those who make some effort to speak German were always rewarded by smiles and a willingness to help.

The Bible got there before us, however: Luke (11: 9-10) tells us "Ask, and it will be given to you; seek, and you will find; knock, and the door will be opened for you. For everyone that asks, receives; and everyone who seeks, finds; and for everyone that knocks the door will be opened." We also know that God will meet us half way: as in the parable of the Prodigal Son, the boy's father is constantly looking for his missing son, and runs to meet him when he is seen returning home. In the same way – however much more trivially – we need to venture forth, to take the initiative; and then we can be secure in the knowledge that we shall be met half way, too.

Points to Ponder

Is initiative dangerous?
Are we too inhibited to go out on a limb?
Is initiative incompatible with our risk-averse society?
Will there always be people ready to criticise when things go wrong
– as they will!

ON LANGUAGE

As a former language teacher I am concerned that the way we use our language should reflect what we want to say: in other words we should try to say what we mean and by extension to mean what we say. Sometimes we obscure our meaning by using what are called circumlocutions – ways to avoid using perhaps offensive words or phrases. I well remember my English master years ago telling us that a blunt speaker was someone who called a spade a spade, rather than a horticultural implement; but that we should perhaps not use the phrase "a b....y shovel".

Sometimes the use of obscure or ambiguous language is deliberate. Years ago a new system for writing references was in use in the United States, called the Lexicon of Inconspicuously Ambiguous Recommendations, or LIAR for short. It included such gems as: "I am pleased to say that this candidate is a former colleague of mine"; or "I most enthusiastically recommend this candidate with no qualifications whatsoever"; or "I would urge you to waste no time in making this candidate an offer of employment". Sometimes we can use a recognised phrase with a new bent: "If you must give this candidate a berth, make it a wide one"; or – one of my favourites from school reports – "He has made an effort; it was one Friday in March"; or, again from a school report from a DT teacher: "Give him the job and he will finish the tools".

There is also the fact that we can communicate meaning by means other than language. We all know what a Frenchman means when he shrugs his shoulders and spreads his hands: he hasn't said a word, but we know that he is telling us that he doesn't know, or perhaps care! We can change the meaning by our tone of voice: "Yes, of *course* I am telling you the truth", and then one would recognise that you were doing no such thing; or again a favourite story of mine about President Nixon, when he was in deep trouble at the time of the Watergate affair. The story goes that his mother phoned him to say: "One thing I have to say, Richard: don't you ever give up!!" His enemies said that what she really said was: "One thing I have to say, Richard: don't you ever give up??"

However, there is another use of language which concerns me far more. When I wandered the playground, on duty or not, I often noticed a quite casual use of bad language. Name-calling is a matter of the misuse of language. Those doing it knew it full well; why otherwise did they pull up short and apologise to me? I would rather they had apologised to those they had abused in this way. I fully appreciate that examples around them and around us do not help: on radio and tv, in the cinema and theatre, and even on billboards in the street, we are surrounded by foul language, until we all become inured to it and – God help us! – it fails any longer to shock us. But shock us it should; or perhaps better, we should be quite grossly offended by those who set out to shock with their infantile ideas of what is clever or funny or humorous. What is worse, from my perspective as a language teacher, is that the free use of such words and phrases deprives anyone of the means of communicating real anger, or disapproval, when the time comes; and that it is a symptom of a lack of better vocabulary, a lack of imagination, to express that anger or disapproval. There is a play, in French, about the seventeenth-century poet Cyrano de Bergerac, who was famed for his long nose. In one scene he is insulted about his nose by a drinking companion; instead of becoming angry, Cyrano rounds on his tormentor, and shows with great self-mockery just how much more telling his comments might have been with the application of a little imagination. And Cyrano does not lose by this encounter: instead his tormentor is forced to leave the inn, to the laughter and jeers of the crowd. So let us mind our tongues; think before we shout; learn some subtlety; and – last but most important – make up our minds what we are really trying to say, about our friends or about anything or anyone else who might, just a little, be getting up *our* nose; and then say it without recourse to bad language or personal abuse.

Points to Ponder

Do you ever feel the necessity to let off steam? Do you indulge in foul language, or do you find more telling ways of expressing yourselves?
Is bad language in fact ever justified?
If so, when?
Would you agree that society's willingness to accept bad language is a large part of the problem?

ON LAUGHTER

Doctors and physiologists tell us that a really good laugh does us a power of good. Indeed, part of the treatment for victims of strokes is to practise laughing again: it seems to strengthen muscles in all parts of the body, and it certainly makes us feel better about ourselves and our world. There is also the old advice that a smile exercises more facial muscles than a frown; it is also much more infectious. It is just as easy to "Spread a little happiness" as to spread gloom and doom; but much better all round.

But what makes you laugh or smile? Do you smile or laugh because you are happy; or because of something funny? What do you find funny? On radio and tv, so much of what now passes for comedy relies heavily on what can only be described as spitefulness, delight in others' discomfort – what the Germans call *Schadenfreude*; or on heavy-handed slapstick – physical comedy; or on the ever-increasing use of bad language. The great giants of comedy, from my childhood, are no more: they found no need for smut or spite, and their altogether gentler approach would perhaps not be understood today, even though people of my generation still find the likes of The Two Ronnies, Morecambe and Wise, Tony Hancock or Kenneth Williams, Joyce Grenfell or Victor Borge quite hilarious. For them situation comedy like *ITMA* – from the war years – or *Take it from here*; or verbal comedy like *Round the Horn* or *Pieces of Eight*; or light-hearted slapstick as practised by Michael Crawford or Norman Wisdom was far more healthy than what now passes for comedy. The best, like the late Harry Secombe, are sometimes described as life-enhancing as they invite us to laugh with them, rather than at them.

I am equally concerned that laughter is often seen as somehow non-pc; that in some way people who laugh are not serious about their work or their relationships or their leisure. Why? It sometimes needs a shaft of humour to defuse a possibly dangerous or unpleasant situation: I have occasionally seen a fight in the playground, which I have stopped by approaching the smallest victim, and telling him to pick on someone his own size – if he can find one! All concerned will see the stupidity of their fight, and stop; perhaps more important, there is no need for the heavy hand of punishment. The same sort of action can puncture the inanity or pomposity of colleagues' ideas, and bring them back to a modicum of common sense. I once upset the headmaster of the time, after he had contrived to time-table me in seven different classrooms, by putting in a request for a Sainsbury's trolley to cart my stuff from one room to the next. I admit that this can often be cruel – laughing others' ideas to scorn is not perhaps the most considerate way to proceed; but sometimes people are impervious to the gentle treatment. But Robert Runcie, who became Archbishop of Canterbury, once said that no-one without a sense of humour ought to be allowed to be in charge of anything.

I come back to ourselves: when we laugh, are we enjoying others' discomfiture? Are we taking pleasure in the distress of another person? Are we lowering ourselves to the level of those whose only source of fun is the use of bad language or dirty jokes? Or is it from the sheer joy of living? Is it because we can share an innocent joke with our friends? Or understand a comical situation for what it is? In a word, are we enjoying the passing pleasure of the moment at someone else's expense, or the deeper and more lasting feeling of happiness?

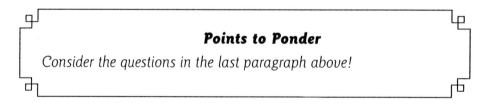

Points to Ponder

Consider the questions in the last paragraph above!

ON LEADERSHIP

What exactly is leadership? Some of us, when we reach the adult world, the world of work, the world of responsibilities, find out what is involved in leadership. Some whilst still at school or college will already have had the opportunity to show whether or not they can lead: as team captains on the sports field, as prefects, as organisers of clubs or societies. A good school, an enlightened school, will try to give pupils the chance to try themselves out in this way. In my time I have seen many young people who possessed the qualities needed, but who were seemingly unaware of the fact until they had been given such an opportunity.

So, what is leadership? Someone once remarked that to be a good leader, you had first to learn how to follow – the implication being that if you could not discipline yourself to accept another's leadership, you had no right to expect others to follow your own lead. There is also the idea that the skills of leadership can be learned from the example of others. Of that I am none too sure: the gift has to be there to start with, even though the ways in which it can be exercised can be learned.

The first quality is perhaps knowledge; a familiarity with the area in which you strive to lead. Teachers we assume, sometimes perhaps unjustifiably, know better than their pupils, more about their particular disciplines; but they must also always be ready to accept that occasionally one of their pupils will be better qualified than they are. There is absolutely nothing wrong with that, for only in that way will progress be made; Newton's comments about his being a pygmy standing on the shoulders of giants come to mind.

But knowledge on its own, while necessary, is not enough. The next, linked closely with it, is authority; not power. Lord Acton reminds us that power corrupts, and for our own times the rider that absolute power corrupts absolutely. For while power can compel, authority will seek to persuade. Leaders, that is good leaders, will not seek to control so much as to inspire, they will seek rather to influence than to rule. The compelled will take the first escape route from that control, while the influenced will live with that inspiration for the rest of their days. Better still, if the example set is a good one they will seek in their turn to influence others in the same way.

Thirdly we should consider charisma – that personal magnetism which can charm even the most level-headed. This is perhaps the most dangerous quality, for many leaders of our times have had charisma in spades, and have then shamefully abused their powers: Hitler is but the most obvious one; he could inspire huge crowds by his rhetoric, without actually saying anything of any real significance.

Next we should think about loyalty, and that is a two-way process, despite so many would-be leaders feeling that they owe no loyalty to their followers. In the armed forces, especially perhaps in war-time, there was an intense bond between leaders and led, between officers and other ranks, an understanding that each would stand by the other in times of difficulty or danger. That level of trust was what marked out men like Mountbatten or Montgomery as true leaders, whose followers would have gone with them to the ends of the earth. Linked with that is an ability to understand the led, a quality which my own Scout leader tried to promote. He asserted that no leader should ask his followers to do anything which he would not have been prepared to do himself in similar circumstances. There is also the corollary that a true leader will not stand in the way of someone who can sensibly push the frontiers forward.

We do not need to look far for a supreme example of leadership: Christ Himself was all of these things. He had authority and knowledge, for we are fairly certain that He spent years studying before His ministry began and we know from the Bible that in argument He was able to run rings round the lawyers and priests in Jerusalem. We know that He was a very charismatic character, able to charm and persuade people of His message. We know that He was intensely loyal to his disciples – even when they let Him down. We know that He was ready to pass on the baton to others, for His Kingdom on Earth would not have been so firmly established without men like Peter and the other Apostles, like Paul and other converts. We know, too, that He established himself with his followers as the servant king: not one who dominated or ordered, but one who shared the menial tasks, who understood the idea of service. There is a couplet from a modern hymn which sums it up quite nicely:

"We strain to glimpse Your mercy-seat,
and find You kneeling at our feet."

(R&S 339)

Do you now want to lead? Can you be such a leader? If so I wish you well.

Points to Ponder

Who are the leaders you would follow?
What qualities do you see in them?
Do you know any real leaders?
What qualities do you most admire in them?
Do you see leadership qualities in yourselves; or in others?
Have you already had the opportunity to lead?
What did you learn from the experience?

ON MIRACLES

What is a miracle? We read in the New Testament of the miracles which Jesus performed: the sceptics say that there is no scientific evidence that such things can happen; the true faithful accept such things on faith; the cautious fall back on *Hamlet*: "there are more things in heaven and earth than are dreamt of in our philosophy". I read once a quotation from *The Voyage*, by Charles Morgan:

> "The sceptical and the credulous, in certain ways they are very alike. It's as if they were living in an enclosed harbour and had forgotten the sea outside. One day the sea flows in strongly; there is an exceptional tide, and one says that it's impossible, that it isn't true; and the other throws up his hands and says that it is a stroke of magic. Both forget the sea outside, and that it is always there and always connected with the water in the harbour; and it is God's mercy that the sea breaks in, or the water in the harbour would stagnate".

There is also the Eastern parable of the elephant in the dark house: men feeling their way in the dark encounter the elephant; one finds an ear and says that it is like a leaf; another finds the trunk and likens it to a snake; a third a leg, which he sees as a tree; a fourth the tusks, which he perceives as spears. All are only partially right; none sees the whole truth.

In less sophisticated times men used the gods to explain the otherwise inexplicable – the god of the gaps. How else could one understand the seasons, the tides, eclipses or earthquakes? In extreme cases sacrifices – humans as well as animals – were needed to placate the angry gods. The ancient Greeks had a god for just about every phenomenon known to humankind; they even went so far as to erect a statue to the "Unknown God" – just in case they had missed one. But with increasing knowledge we came to see that such ideas were mere superstition, as we found more rational explanations; and with that growth of understanding we rejected the idea of miracles. In so doing, however, we also took on board the idea that anything which could not be explained scientifically simply could not happen: many scientists, particularly in the materialistic period between the two world wars, also rejected the idea of God, or of religion. Nowadays many scientists accept quite willingly the notion of an omnipotent Creator: there is too much order and beauty in the Universe for it to have emerged at random.

But to come back to our quotation – and to *Hamlet*: there is always the possibility that there are natural laws, yet to be discovered, which will explain the as yet inexplicable. Can we believe that God, even an omnipotent God, would suspend the natural laws which He has put in place? Is not the main miracle that we have been given the insatiable curiosity to explore our Universe, and to try to make sense of it? One must, however, be aware of the dangers of what the ancient Greeks called *hubris*, that over-weening pride, the danger of setting ourselves up as equal to God, simply because we have managed to explain some of his miracles. It was in ancient times always followed by *nemesis*, when the gods had a nasty knack of catching up with such arrogance.

There is another dimension to the concept of miracles. I once heard of a Catholic primary school, one class of which had planted out some boxes of seeds, as part of the nature study course. The seeds seemed to be languishing in the classroom; so the children had the idea of placing the boxes in the school's foyer, under a statue of the Virgin Mary. Lo and behold, the seeds began to sprout most vigorously. A miracle, thought the children. Not so, said the caretaker: one of the cleaners had taken to watering the boxes each evening, and the warmer air of the foyer had encouraged faster and better growth. Should we tell the children? No, said the teacher – let them believe a little longer in miracles. I also heard one of those silly stories in which there is a grain of wisdom: it concerned a priest in a valley which was about to be inundated by a flood. So great was the flood that the villagers had to take refuge on the roofs of their houses. The rescue services took rowing boats round to save the villagers – all except the priest, who said that he would wait for God's miracle. When finally the waters rose to overwhelm him, he called to God, demanding to know why he had not been saved. God replied: "Why did you not accept the help that I sent you?"

Another quotation: "Jesus never asked anyone to do a job without showing them how. When they thought they were out of loaves and fishes, He provided; when they were out of hope, He provided; when the wine was exhausted, He provided. That was His business: He showed that the impossible was possible and that, with God's blessing added, miracles can happen.....that ordinary people could undertake extraordinary journeys".

Can we go out today, this week, every day and every week, determined to do our little bit to help God perform his miracles?

Points to Ponder

How can we define a miracle?
Are miracles possible in a sceptical age?
Will science eventually be able to explain all "miracles"?
Are we all in fact capable of performing miracles?

ON OPTIMISM

It is said that the optimist sees the half-full glass, while the pessimist sees the half-empty one – it depends on one's point of view. The French writer Voltaire wrote many years ago about a man he called Pangloss, who believed that all was for the best in the best of all possible worlds; which inspired a much later writer to say that the optimist believes that this is the best of all possible worlds, while the pessimist believes that he may well be right. Some people argue that if we are pessimistic we cannot be disappointed and indeed it may well be that things will often turn out better than we expected. So why should we be optimistic? Do we have any reason to think that the best will happen?

Too often we are persuaded that it is only sensible and realistic to expect the worst of other people. That sort of low expectation is very contagious: it leads us all to think the worst of our fellows, to expect inconsiderate or selfish behaviour, to see nothing surprising in criminal or dangerous actions, to take dishonesty and stupidity as the norm. And so we enter a downward spiral of despair, a vicious spiral, which one can escape only with a great deal of effort.

The odd thing is that if we expect the best sometimes it really happens. This is especially true of people: if we expect others to behave badly, they will; while if we expect the best, more often than not they will respond to these more positive thoughts, and behave rather better. The German writer Goethe put it quite neatly: "When we take man as he is, we make him worse; but when we take man as if he were already what he should be, we promote him to what he can be". There is something quite infectious about the more cheerful way of viewing the world: if we can put behind us the destructive and cynical ways which pass for worldly wisdom, and adopt the more happy-go-lucky ways of the fool, the naïve, the unworldly, miracles will often happen.

Too often we can be misled by the newspapers – whose business is after all to report the news. Good news is often no news at all: *News at Ten*, as it was then, made a point of finishing its nightly bulletins with a piece of good news; and gave up the effort after a very short time – no-one wanted to know. But some years ago, when this country was going through a very rough patch, someone wrote a strong letter to the press, in which he argued that we should celebrate the Year of the Normal. In the coming year, he said, most workers would get by without striking; most housewives would survive without recourse to Valium; most children would be able to resist the temptation to assault their teachers; most policemen would refrain from falsifying their evidence or beating up their suspects; most parents would succeed in bringing up their children without resorting to child-abuse or over-permissiveness; a few politicians might occasionally tell the truth.

He went on to say that the "normal", the "optimistic", needed to band together to make the most of their strength, to put across the idea that life is a joy, to be taken as it comes; that constantly banging on about rights without responsibilities, (and how familiar that sounds) does not bring happiness or contentment; that fighting one's own corner with scant concern for others is not the be all and end all of human existence. As so often, St Paul got there before us: in his letter to the Philippians he enjoined us: "Finally, brethren, whatever is true, whatever is honourable, whatever is just, whatever is pure, whatever is lovely, whatever is pleasing: if there is any excellence and if there is anything worthy of praise, think about these things." Can we all – New Year or not – take a rather more positive view of life, and of our ability to influence it for good?

Points to Ponder
Are we too often tempted to take the pessimistic view?
How infectious can optimism be?
"Laugh and the world laughs with you; cry and you cry alone".

ON PATIENCE

We live in age when things seem to moving ever faster, and in an age when to wait for things is out of fashion. When I married, it was the norm that engagements were a period for building the partnership, and for accumulating some of the material possessions that the new household would need. It was accepted that the new household would not start out with everything needed for a comfortable life. The newly-wed young couple were expected to work for the things they needed or wanted; their in-laws were on hand to make sure that things did not go too sadly amiss; and that working together, that sense of collaboration between husband and wife, was often the cement which kept the marriage going. Nowadays young people, if indeed they get married at all, expect a fully-furnished home, with all mod cons. The result too often seems to be that the couple have no common aim, nothing to work for or strive for; so that when the partnership hits a rough patch, and this will inevitably happen to every such partnership, there is no "glue" to hold it together until better times arrive.

When I was at school one of the set books we had to read for 'A' Level was *Hamlet*. Hamlet's tragedy was that he delayed – he dithered perhaps because he could not make up his mind to do what he really thought was necessary; he looked constantly for reasons not to take action; he might have been a dreamer, not cut out for the destiny which his birth might have mapped out for him; he might well have been a coward, fearing the consequences of actions foreign to him. Only towards the end of the play, when he sees his own death staring him in the face, does he take the plunge, and avenge his father. That is not really the sort of patience which should commend itself to anyone.

Job, in the Old Testament, is a different story entirely, and his patience is now proverbial. An exemplary man, upright in all his dealings with God and man, Job is handed by God to Satan, who then visits all manner of sufferings and loss upon the poor man, in the hope of proving that his faith in God is only superficial. Satan loses his "bet" with God, with Job remaining steadfast in his faith even in the most appalling circumstances.

The opposite of such patience might be described as divine discontent. Most of us, when faced with such sufferings as afflicted Job, would do our best to put things right for ourselves. We might well moan while we are doing so, but it is far better, and it is also no contradiction of the idea of patience, to make the best of a bad job and to try to improve matters. We all face the need for such patience every day, and parents and teachers know that the long processes whereby you turn from unformed children into responsible and reliable adults are often a test, sometimes a very sore test of patience.

To conclude, may I recommend the prayer for patience:

God grant me the courage to change the things I can change;
the serenity to accept the things I cannot change;
and the wisdom to know the difference between them.

Points to Ponder

Can impatience be justified? If so, in what circumstances?
Is patience the same thing as passivity?
Do we sometimes try to excuse angry frustration by calling it impatience?

ON PRAYER

It is one of the oldest instincts of thinking man to pray. In early man's psyche – long before the emergence of priests and "holy men" – there was lodged the idea that there were powers over and above anything that men on their own could muster. In time these powers, the weather, the sun and moon, the seasons, became "personified": they were made into gods who demanded prayers and sacrifices if they were to be persuaded not to wreak vengeance on hapless mankind. Because of the simple nature of men and women of the time, such prayers could be proved by the holy men to "work" if the prayers were coincidentally answered; and so the concept of gods and goddesses was allowed to develop. It also allowed the "holy men" to impose – often very sensible – ideas about behaviour and practices, holding that they were the wishes of the gods of the tribe.

We are supposed now to be more sophisticated; and many people in our own times will be quite scornful of the idea of praying, whether to the gods of the ancients or to our own God, Christian, Jewish, Muslim or that of any other of the many religions which profess a belief in a Supreme Being. Such people believe that man alone is responsible for what happens to him, and that God – or the gods – can have no influence over his fate. Christians, on the other hand, can believe that while people must take responsibility for their own actions, a belief in God can help to steer things.

I once came across a useful acrostic to remind us why we pray – and it is significant that the Lord's Prayer contains in such concise form all four elements: they are **A**doration; **C**onfession; **T**hanksgiving; and **S**upplication; or **ACTS** for short. All these elements are needed, and the psychologists tell us that these four acts help us to be at peace with ourselves and by extension with others around us.

We need, even so, to be realistic in our prayers, especially in those of supplication: we see a house on fire, and there is little point in asking for the fire to be extinguished; but there is everything to be gained by praying that no-one should be hurt by the fire. These are what might be termed short-term wishes, the sort that even the non-religious among us might concede. Someone once said, at the time of the First World War, that there are no atheists in the trenches! When that faith persists we may all rejoice: Jesus told us (Luke 18: 1-8) that we must persist in our prayer and not be downcast. He also warned us (vv 9-14) that we must be sincere and humble, and indeed private, in our devotions.

Christians, too, believe in the effectiveness of prayer: all too often we hear of people who recover from illness, or feel at peace with their problems, after prayers are offered for them; *even when they are not aware of the fact!* When we pray for ourselves, we often find that we are granted a solution to a problem, even if it might not be the obvious one. Often our prayers are granted, again in ways which we would not have considered. As has been remarked, God always answers our prayers – even if the answer is often "No!"

But there is another side to the question of prayer. Often we hear people say of another's actions: "You are the answer to my prayer!" Can you be sensitive to others' needs in this way? Can you be there when they need help or support?

Points to Ponder

Do you pray; or meditate?
Do you see prayer as a religious duty,
or as a natural part of man's behaviour?
Does prayer work?
Are there any instances in your own life of a prayer being answered?
Do you find answers or solutions emerging after prayer or meditation?

ON REBELLION

The average teenager is a rebellious individual. He or she, (there is no discrimination in this particular feature of life), is learning the ways of the world; and the world, if it has any sense, is putting some quite strict limits on the behaviour of its young people. Some of those young people probably feel some resentment towards adults for the way in which they place restrictions which all too often appear to be negative. That resentment will sometimes explode in fits of temper, tantrums, sullenness; all those weapons of teenage disapproval. They – quite rightly – want to pitch themselves against the world, to show their mettle, to find their rightful place in the pecking order. They want to see how strong they can be; and again responsible adults will seek to show the limits of what is acceptable in a social context. In many ways adults do teenagers no service if they fail to set those limits, for they fail also to give a framework within which it is safe to operate and for everyone to find their rightful place.

To a limited extent school rules try to set that context. Most schools will have rules which show how pupils should behave towards each other, towards the school's authority, and thence towards society. Some of those rules will seem trivial, almost insulting in their assumption·that they cannot behave like civilised human beings. One reason might be that, while they are working out ways of circumventing the comparatively harmless rules, they are not doing themselves much worse harm by pushing at the limits. Teachers owe it to pupils to show how far they may safely go and if need be by punishing them if they exceed those limits.

So why do people, especially young people, rebel? Here we need to ask ourselves a serious question, and to give it a serious and well-considered answer. Do they rebel simply in order to shock others, who, let us be honest, are often easily shocked? Or do they rebel because they wish to challenge assumptions, complacency, or thoughtlessness? If the former, they could be wasting their energy and a real opportunity; for, though the others may be easily shocked, they are also often rather too long in the tooth to take the 'rebels' seriously, and to take them at their own valuation. If the latter, however, they will be doing both themselves and other people real service; for long held assumptions may be no longer valid in a rapidly-changing world. There should be a sort of social contract between the young and rebellious who are the world's future, and those have some knowledge of the ways of the world. The generation gap may be a nice tidy notion for the rebel who wishes simply to be noticed; it is not so useful for the constructive rebel. Adults should be prepared to listen to what youngsters have to say as long as it is constructive; and they should also be prepared to engage in useful dialogue. Only in this way can the enthusiasm of youth be harnessed with the wisdom – such as it may be – of maturity. I would personally set just three conditions: that young people should know what they are talking about, for there is nothing worse than having the ground cut from under their feet simply because the facts have not been checked; that they should be able to accept that sometimes they do not have enough experience of the world to make sweeping statements; and that they should always, but always, be courteous in their dealings with others. There is nothing to be gained from abuse and belligerence – except the suspicion that the perpetrator is so very, very wrong.

I may upset other teachers when I say that I preferred my pupils to be rebellious, I preferred them to take me on in argument, and I preferred them to exercise their rebelliousness against me. At least in that way they were engaging me in that fruitful dialogue which is the only way in which any progress will be made. Adults are perhaps accustomed to being always in the right; but it is not always so. My scout leader, so many years ago, was quite clear in his own mind that the collective wisdom of the boys in his troop was greater than his own; by giving us our heads in argument he allowed us to hone our arguments, and our argumentative skills, and also to convince him that he was hopelessly out of touch with modern realities. It is a wise teacher who can accept that just occasionally some of his or her pupils will prove to be way ahead of their mentors.

May I leave you with the thought that everyone must give close thought to the reasons for their rebellious natures, and how energies might be best harnessed to the betterment of society. For young people it will soon be their world, to do with as they may think best.

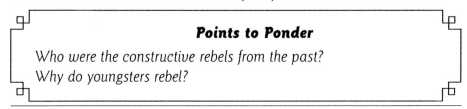

Points to Ponder

Who were the constructive rebels from the past?
Why do youngsters rebel?

ON REDEMPTION

One or two of you might be familiar with the story from Greek legend of Orestes, who came home from his wanderings to find that his mother had murdered his father in order that she might marry her lover. Orestes avenged his father's death by killing his mother. For the ancient Greeks there was nothing really so terrible about a woman's murdering her husband; but a man – or any child: Orestes' sisters were also involved – murdering his parents, which involved the blood tie, was quite another matter. It was subject to the vengeance of the Furies, who in this legend pursued Orestes to insanity and to death. An updated version of the story, *Les Mouches*, by the French writer Sartre, has the Furies personified in a plague of flies, which will leave the city only when Orestes himself departs. The older story of Oedipus is rather similar: at the time of his birth it was foretold that he would kill his father and marry his mother. These events came about; and the Furies pursued him in like fashion, driving him to leave his family and his city, to become a mendicant and to blind himself. In both cases the main character of the legend, having sinned most grievously, has to make amends and has to redeem himself.

Most of us know that when we have been subjected to some insult or injury, we will moan about it, we will take our revenge, sometimes on our tormentor, but more often on someone not originally involved who is less able to defend himself; we will seek some way of making ourselves feel "better" about things. But it does not work: in this way the whole miserable business continues, one ripple which extends itself to embrace us all in bitterness, hatred, violence, resentment. What it needs is an acknowledgement by the original offender that he or she has done wrong, together with a plea for forgiveness. That is a lot to ask, possibly too much in these days where it is almost unknown for anyone to admit to anything, let alone to ask for pardon. It therefore falls to the one sinned against to make the first move. I do not believe that forgiveness works properly unless the offender is prepared to ask for it; but a gracious refusal on the part of the "victim" to retaliate is the next best thing.

This quality of redemption is at the core of Christian belief. The Catholic Mass refers to Jesus as the Lamb of God, who takes away the sins of the world. If you like, Jesus puts up his own notice, saying: "The buck stops here". He invited us: "Come to Me, all ye that labour and are heavy laden and I will give you rest". He will listen to our complaints, will patiently put up with our petty grumblings, will suffer the outbursts of our vengeful tempers. He will guarantee no violence in return, he will take it all to God, and will be the buffer which will absorb all the bitterness which we need to purge from our souls. And by leaving the city – our world – as he did, he undertakes also to deliver us from the plague which besets us; even though he was no sinner. That is the true meaning of redemption: Christ made himself the sacrifice on whom the Furies would fix their attention, that the rest of us might live in peace and freedom.

Points to Ponder

Why do people not accept that they have offended?

Why do those offended against find it difficult to take the first step?

Have you been in the position of having offended and of being unable to admit the fact?

Have you been in the position of having been offended, and of being unable to refrain from retaliation?

ON REMEMBRANCE DAY I

Some years ago, on the way home from the school's annual visit to Normandy, we called in at the Peace Memorial at Caen. An impressive piece of work, it sets out to bring to notice the events leading up to the last war, the war itself and the events since. I noticed that several of the boys were visibly affected by what they saw here; but I myself found the visit profoundly depressing and indeed distressing. There were really three main reasons for this.

When one enters the memorial, one descends a long shallow ramp from the ground level into the basement. The walls are lined with photos, documents, newspapers – all evidence of the extent to which no-one wanted war, but also showing how far the actions of the politicians of those days had exactly the opposite effect to that intended; and thereby made war inevitable.

The second source of my discomfort, much more real for me, lay in the basement displays. Here we saw some of the weapons of war: some boys asked me about a peculiar sausage-shaped weapon with a small propeller on the back. These were known as doodle-bugs – semi-guided rockets. Their horrific chugging sound as they crossed London is one of the abiding memories from my early childhood: I remember standing one evening at home in the back garden, to see one of these rockets pass overhead. The engine cut out as we watched, and that was the time to take cover, for it would now fall, perhaps on to a house nearby. The thud and explosion from that particular rocket came less than a minute later, as it fell nearly two miles away. I still have cold shivers when I hear the eerie wail of the old air raid sirens, or see searchlights in the night sky.

The third reason for distress is in what has happened in the years since that war ended. I grew up in the forties and fifties with the ever-present threat of a new war, and with the menace of nuclear weapons to face too. It nearly happened on several occasions, most notably during the Berlin blockade, when the Russians forbade any sort of road or rail transport into the city. For a year everything the Berliners wanted had to be flown in

– the famous Luftbrücke: coal, raw materials for industry, even water, let alone food and clothing. The Korean war broke out in the fifties: there was every chance that, when I was eventually called up for my two years in the Forces, I would be sent out there. In the event that war ended in 1954; but when I did finally join up in 1956 the Suez war had been over for a matter of weeks. The barracks where I was posted still had tanks lined up ready, with their sand-coloured camouflage. Despite the best efforts of the United Nations, NATO and the rest, someone has calculated that the world has been fully at peace for a total of about thirty days in the past half-century; and that at any one time there have been as many as ten separate conflicts in progress across the globe.

The children I taught never had to face a real war and please God they never will. It is not a glamorous matter: one of the jobs I had to do as a young civil servant was to wind up the Far East Prisoners of War Fund. At the end of the war the Burma-Siam railway – the story is told in the film *The Bridge over the River Kwai* – was sold off, and the proceeds used to compensate those prisoners of war who had suffered so cruelly during its building. The accounts that I had to read, of the sufferings of those prisoners of war, were harrowing; and even twenty years after the event these men – and women and children – were still suffering horribly from the privations of those years. We have seen in newspapers and on TV what is going on in Africa, in Sri Lanka, in the Middle East, in Bosnia, in Northern Ireland or in Afghanistan – to name but a few. All these conflicts have come about, not because the ordinary man in the street wanted them to happen, but because leaders, through short-sighted folly, greed, selfishness or sheer ineptitude, allowed them to happen. There are such things as just wars: when real injustices, real horrors are seen to be happening, one has to fight to ensure that they do not persist. But in so doing we run the risk of other outrages; and we need to be on ever-vigilant guard to make sure that we keep to the right path.

Recently we have reinstituted the celebration of Remembrance on its true date, the 11th November. When I began working in Westminster one of the most moving memories was of the whole of London, indeed of the whole country, coming to a halt for the two minutes' silence; and of the eerie quiet that used to descend on the capital. In those days men still raised their hats as they passed the Cenotaph; and servicemen of all ranks were required to salute. Such marks of respect are nowadays regarded as unacceptable – we are now expected to be far too politically correct to demean ourselves in this way. But I have always held that we demean ourselves, and those who deserve our consideration, by *not* showing that respect.

Points to Ponder

Will we ever truly eradicate war? Are there other ways
of resolving the conflicts which have led to war in the past?
Is any purpose served by continually remembering past conflicts?

ON REMEMBRANCE DAY II

Today is the eleventh day of November; and at one time Remembrance Day would have been commemorated this morning, with a full-scale parade in Central London and the traditional two minutes' silence at eleven o'clock. Now, after a period when it was considered too inconvenient to disrupt London in this way, we are back to the practice of two minutes silence, and perhaps this is a time when such acts of remembrance are once more only too necessary. With the passage of time memory fades: those with personal recollections of the horrors of the war die, leaving those who wish to forget, or who have never had the dubious honour of experiencing those horrors. Why therefore remember?

Perhaps, so that such horrors as are brought about by war may never be repeated. The danger these days is that there is a tendency, especially on tv, to glamorise warfare, and to gloss over the pain, the suffering and the deprivation which are the other side of the full picture. I have sometimes quoted Konrad Lorenz and others who believe that assertiveness is an integral and indeed vital part of the human psyche. What *none* of them say is that assertive attitudes must necessarily find violent expression. No psychologist in my own reading has ever tried to argue that war is an unavoidable part of the human condition – even when we seem so often to fall back on it. But the will to sublimate aggression, to find harmless outlets for its expression, will be lacking unless we see, and *remember*, its consequences.

When I was a teacher I thanked God that war was well out of the experience of my pupils; and it was expecting too much of them to ask them to imagine what it is like – even for those with ambitions to join the Forces. My uncle died in the trenches in 1916, at the tender age of 21, in the messiest way possible, by an attack of chlorine gas. The filth and mud of the trenches in that war are still legendary, matched only by the misery and degradation of humanity suffered during the World War 2. I once met a man who, more than thirty years later, was still suffering from what is called shellshock – a state of nervous collapse due to the incessant explosion of bombs, shells, ammunition. I have taken groups of young people to war cemeteries across Europe, in Bayeux, in Berlin, in Stuttgart and they have all been appalled at the age at which some of the victims died. One, at Bayeux, was only 16. We have visited the Mémorial de la Paix at Caen – a visit which, while among the most depressing that I can remember, should be compulsory. And there are still many people existing, it can hardly be called living, deprived of limbs, of mobility, of senses, even of personality. To quote a British Legion poster: "The memory fades, but the suffering doesn't".

But there is a positive side to war too. If you go to London, and look up Charing Cross Road from outside St Martin's in the Fields, you will see a statue. On it are carved the words: "Patriotism is not enough; I must have no hatred or bitterness for anyone". They were the last recorded words of Nurse Edith Cavell, who devoted her skill and energies to all who needed them, regardless of nationality. She was shot in 1915 by the Germans for allegedly helping some two hundred Allied soldiers to escape to Holland. And countless men and women, in both world wars and in all the other interminable local squabbles before and since, have demonstrated their belief in the one-ness of mankind, and have tried to alleviate the misery caused by political pigheadedness and stupidity.

Peace is the dream of everyone, through all ages; it is the basis of the world's great religions. At a Remembrance Day service one year we sang one of the famous Christmas carols – about the angels' message of peace to the world. So why do we fight? War can sometimes be avoided by diplomacy: some people feel that the Second World War and, much later, the Falklands conflict could have been avoided by a better understanding of each other's point of view. But was Saddam Hussein open to reason? Was Hitler? Are the savages who massacred tourists at Luxor, or those who regularly killed and maimed on the streets of Northern Ireland? Such acts bring us the concept of the just war, where a problem can be solved only by excising the poison.

However much we may long for peace, it still has to be worked at. It is often said that alone one can do nothing. Not true. Staff try to stop bullying in school; and only rightly so. But can the bullies stop themselves indulging in bullying? If so, they have taken one small step down the road of peace. We need to learn the habits of peace: tolerance, reason, quiet argument and persuasion, influence – so much more powerful than force, for force can be counter-productive when those who have been forced to adopt a point of view give it up once the force is removed.

One of the most powerful poems about war was written by Col John McCrae during the Battle of the Somme in 1915:

> In Flanders fields the poppies blow,
> Between the crosses, row on row,
> That mark our place; and in the sky
> The larks, still bravely singing, fly
> Scarce heard amid the guns below.
>
> We are the Dead: short days ago
> We lived, felt dawn, saw sunset glow,
> Loved and were loved; and now we lie
> In Flanders fields.
>
> Take up our quarrel with the foe.
> To you from ailing hands we throw
> The Torch; be yours to hold it high.
> If ye break faith with us who die
> We shall not sleep, though poppies grow
> In Flanders fields.

Points to Ponder

Will we ever truly eradicate war?
Are there other ways of resolving the conflicts which have led to war in the past?
Is any purpose served by continually remembering past conflicts?

ON RESPECT

Rules are framed on the premise that we should have due regard for others; and civilisation could not properly function if we simply followed our own selfish desires. In school I often tried to put across the idea that if we are to live together we have to surrender some of our freedom to act just as we wish, in the interests of a quiet life for us all. But there is also the vexed question of respect, which has unfortunately become bound up with the idea that to show respect to others is somehow to demean oneself, and that respect simply means a show of grovelling deference. That is sheer nonsense. There is a world of difference between the grovelling of say Uriah Heap, which had nothing of respect in it, and the healthy respect which we owe each other as a matter of course. Let's consider the respect which we all have to earn from each other.

Firstly, we are encouraged to learn to respect those having authority – but without perhaps understanding what authority is. Do we respect those who are authoritative – who know what they are talking about, because they know more than we do? Or do we respect those who are authoritarian – because they are stronger than us, or because they have the weight of oppressive rule behind them? The first is healthy, because the respect which we give is not only deserved but also voluntary; but the second is not respect at all, but fear, and those who claim to command respect in this way do not perhaps perceive the difference. Those who have aspirations to be leaders, in any field, need to learn that difference. Secondly, we learn to respect others because of their personal qualities such as honesty or trustworthiness or compassion; or not to respect them because those qualities are lacking. Lastly, we learn to respect others simply because they are also members of the human race: it is quite possible to fail to respect others because they are not respectable, because they are lacking qualities which command our respect, and at the same time respect them simply for existing, for living alongside ourselves.

In so many ways this has to do with courtesy, again an outmoded concept among those who suffer so much from an inferiority complex that in-your-face aggression is the only way to patch their damaged characters. Someone once described courtesy as the lubricant which keeps society running smoothly: one has only to see what happens when the social conventions break down. I read recently of a man who, at a tennis club, broke the convention which dictates that one does not walk across a court when a point is being played. On being reminded of this convention, the man simply retorted: "No-one tells *me* what to do!". Courtesy, and the well-established rituals which enable us to rely on others to behave decently and of course they on us, do make life much more bearable. In a crowded and tightly-knit community such conventions are not simply polite; they become a way of enabling us to live together in something approaching harmony, and to display a proper and healthy respect to others – *all* others.

Points to Ponder

Can we legislate for respect?
If not, how do we teach the need for respect, and how to exercise respect for others?
Who are the people you respect?
Why do you respect them?

ON RESPONSIBILITY

The Parable of the Talents (Matthew 25: 14-30) is a very dense parable, full of hidden meanings. I would like to consider just one of those hidden meanings.

Some time ago a woman in America suffered a rather nasty accident when she spilled a cup of hot coffee over herself. She had just bought the coffee at McDonald's, and decided to sue the company for not warning her that hot coffee can be – well – hot. In similar vein a man ventured out – during a storm – on to the jetty at Weymouth; and then sued the local council for not having erected warning signs. More recently a bank robber in Germany sued the manager of his victim bank. The thief, it appears, was deaf; the bank manager realised this, and saw that there would be no danger in sounding the alarm. The grounds for the suing: that the manager had quite callously taken advantage of the thief's physical disabilities.

There is a distressing tendency nowadays to try to blame others, any others, for our misfortunes. Sometimes these misfortunes are quite unavoidable; we have to learn to live with them, or find ways of ameliorating or removing their causes. Occasionally blame can be quite easily fixed; and in such cases it is only right that those to blame be held responsible. However in the vast majority of cases we ourselves make at least a contribution to our woes; and to try to take refuge by foisting the blame on others is at the very least dishonest. All three of the cases I cited just now fall into that category.

The story of the ten talents is often told to illustrate our duty to make the best of the gifts with which we have been endowed. Let's consider how the King was prepared to give his servants a measure of responsibility. Two of them performed well; and the King was pleased and proud. But the third ducked his responsibility, whether from laziness or timidity, we shall never know; and the King was not at all pleased.

In many ways the story illustrates what happens in a school. Most schools, some more successfully than others, try to provide opportunities for young people to take a small measure of responsibility: charity representatives; form captains; sports captains; secretaries for clubs; prefects and so on. There is one difference: the staff know that some will fail; will stumble; will feel happier not taking on these burdens. However they do not throw the pupils into the outer darkness, as happened to the third servant. They are there to pick up the pieces, provide a shoulder to cry on – all in the hope that the young people will emerge from the experience stronger, more able to pick up the challenge, and will be willing and able to try again. Failure is nothing to be ashamed of – in the words of a wise man, he who never made a mistake never made anything; in the words of another wise man, the only failure is to give up trying.

Everyone should take opportunities: never pass up the chance to take responsibility – more especially when so many around want to prevent you from doing so! There is a pride to be taken in not having to rely unnecessarily on anyone else. Indeed having learned ourselves we may be in the fortunate position of being able to help others to grow in the same fashion.

Points to Ponder

Do you hold any positions of responsibility?
Could you rise to the challenge of responsibility?
If so, what would be your chosen field?
Or would you duck it?
If so, why?

ON RISK-TAKING

In the news recently we read about the way in which children are increasingly prone to such ailments as asthma because, and only because, they have been brought up in a sterile ultra-hygienic environment. In other words their ability to strengthen their immune systems has been weakened because, and only because, they have not been exposed to danger, dirt, disease. Childish illnesses are much less dangerous if contracted in childhood, and the patients will in this way have their immunity to such diseases well established. Those who do not have such immunity may well fall ill in adulthood, when the dangers are much greater.

We heard also recently about achievement, about striving to be the best that you can be, for your own satisfaction as well as for the good of your fellows. But that striving will inevitably involve risk-taking: whatever you strive to do, to improve on what has gone before, to initiate, to innovate, you lay yourself open to risk, to danger.

Such dangers are not now thought to be politically correct: there are too many people around who would deprive others of the opportunity to test themsleves in this way; and this nannying tendency, this almost fascist desire of too many to control what the rest of us do is, to me, a very worrying feature of our life today. Young people in particular have the almost insatiable desire to test themselves; if that desire is stifled there will always be trouble – for young people are also naturally revolting. Most schools have among their "Aims and Objectives" the desire to produce young people who are strong, self-reliant, independent, worthy citizens. I once got myself into trouble in one school for pointing out that, even if these were the aims, little was being done to bring them about. These goals will not be reached unless teachers are prepared to let pupils take risks: they can learn from experience, from trial-and-error, even from making mistakes – especially when they can be confident that there will be someone there to help to pick up the pieces. Some years ago Sweden came to the inconvenient conclusion that its government's policy of cradle-to-grave security was fundamentally mistaken. Perhaps not coincidentally, the suicide rate in Sweden at that time was far higher than in similarly developed nations. There was the suspicion that removing risk also removed the need to strive; and that if there was nothing to fight for, there was little point in living.

Taking risks is a fundamental and vital feature of any living organism: we are taking risks from the day we are born to the day we die. Without it there can be no progress, no improvement; and it is an important part of our function as adults to help young people to prepare to take risks sensibly. As a Scout leader I took risks, some rather more foolhardy than others! But I learned my craft under the watchful eye of more experienced adults, who could and would guide me if – or rather more often when – I was too far off beam. Thus I learned how to take calculated risks; and much more importantly, when not to. In Scotland one New Year's holiday, I wanted to take a party across Rannoch Moor, which is not the most hospitable area under a good sun, and decidedly dangerous under a few feet of snow. An older man drove us up there; but said nothing. Before we reached our planned starting point I had decided that this was sheer foolishness; but I felt much better for having been allowed to decide for myself and my party, rather than having a more experienced leader forbid me. On the same trip we had a young man who was quite wild. On one occasion, out on the mountain and in deep snow conditions, he acted so erratically that he was a danger to himself and to the rest of his party; and he had to be sent home. In both cases there were risks which were not worth taking.

In the same way, when I led parties from school, to Normandy, to Berlin, or ski parties to Switzerland or America, I took risks. I often had to ask myself, should I really be taking this "character" abroad? Will that youngster really benefit from this trip? Thankfully, in very few cases I felt strongly enough to say no to a pupil; thankfully too, I was very seldom let down when I said yes. As Head of Department I had to take risks, with new courses, new syllabuses, even new colleagues. When such ventures did not work I was rapped over the knuckles; when they did no-one seemed to notice! Whatever may be the reaction of those in charge, however, we still need intrepid souls who will dare, who will rise to the challenges, who will politely tell those who would hinder them to stand back.

I would like to give you two quotations: the first is "Security is mostly a superstition. It does not exist in nature, nor do the children of men as a whole experience it. Avoiding danger is no safer in the long run than outright exposure. Life is either a daring adventure, or it is nothing." The second is pithier: "A ship in harbour is safe; but that is not what ships are built for."

My message is therefore, take the ball and run with it; aim high, for if you do not aim, you cannot expect to hit anything. It may not work out; in which case you, and you alone, will have to learn to live with the feeling of failure. But more often than not it will; and then your sense of achievement will be enormous. Go to it!

Points to Ponder

Have you ever done anything risky?
Did you feel justified in taking those risks?
Did you succeed, or fail?
If you failed, who was in your view to blame?
What did you learn in the process?
How do we learn to distinguish between justifiable and unjustifiable risks?

ON SERVICE

When the House of Lords was in effect abolished, the excuse used at the time was that it was outmoded, undemocratic, an affront to a modern democracy; all this despite the fact that it was often very much more in tune with the wishes of the people than was the House of Commons. We live in an age when accountability is the watchword, and the Lords were not accountable in the way that the Commons, or our local councils, are accountable. We also live in times when it seems that we value only what we can pay for – and conversely feel that we must pay for what we value.

But this is not a political statement. I am more concerned with what we have lost through this act of cheap vandalism, the idea of service, unpaid, unsung, too often unrecognised, almost always unacknowledged. We talk glibly of vocation, the sense that one is called to a particular activity, without perhaps seeing that it was just that – vocation – which led people down the years to do those tasks which needed doing: for it was the Churches in the main which set up the first hospitals, the first schools, the first welfare services. This was not because the Government decreed it; not because there was a democratic vote on it; not because the taxpayer was willing to fund it; but simply because enlightened people recognised a need and worked to meet it. That work was often dirty, often messy, often unpleasant; so therefore the need for a vocation was even stronger.

But there was also the idea of *noblesse oblige* – the notion that those who were born to a privileged life, with greater wealth, or talent, or strength, or time, should feel under some obligation to come to the aid of those less well-endowed. We now decry the idea that our nobility have any intrinsic value; we are quite simply unaware, possibly for reasons of political correctness, that many noblemen and women worked hard to provide gainful employment, or means of self-improvement, or opportunities for education, for those under their occasionally cruel, but far more often benign protection.

We have now grown away from this idea of service. The cry is always for the Government to "do something". But the Churches are still there, and for all their weakness are still having an effect on our lives. Several years ago there was the movement for Christian Stewardship, where church members were urged to give not only of their treasure, but also of their time and talents for the greater good. Albert Schweitzer, a noted doctor who was also a gifted organist, and who could have made a great name for himself in either field, chose to give it all up to work in a tiny African town called Lambarene, supported only by charitable giving. He said once that we should all regard giving a portion of our spare time and talent to the service of others as a real duty: he said:

"I have always held firmly to the thought that each one of us can do a little to bring some portion of misery to an end".

On another occasion he said:

"Reverence for life does not allow the scholar to live for his science alone, even if he is very useful to the community in so doing; or the artist to exist only for his art, even if he gives inspiration to many. It refuses to let the businessman imagine that he fulfils all legitimate demands in the course of his business activities. It demands from all that they should sacrifice a portion of their own lives for others".

A man called Stephen Grellet some two hundred years ago wrote in similar vein:

"I expect to pass through this world but once; any good thing therefore that I can do, or any kindness that I can show to a fellow-creature, let me do it now; let me not defer or neglect it, for I shall not pass this way again."

Here are two thing which sum up what service means: first a couple of verses from a modern hymn

We are pilgrims on a journey,
and companions on the road;
we are here to help each other
walk the mile and bear the load.

I will weep when you are weeping;
when you laugh I'll laugh with you;
I will share your joy and sorrow
till we've seen this journey through.

(R&S 474)

And secondly a prayer:

Teach us, good Lord, to serve Thee as Thou deservest: to give and not
to count the cost; to fight and not to heed the wounds; to toil and not
to seek for rest; to labour and not to ask for any reward, save that of
knowing that we do Thy will.

Points to Ponder

Have you already undertaken some kind of community service?
If so, in which field?
Do you appreciate the need for service of this sort?
Or should the Government or some other public body instead do all
that is necessary?
Can the Government in fact do everything in this way?

ON SOCIAL OUTCASTS

I once came across this, during a Christian Aid Week campaign:

*I was hungry; and you formed a discussion group to discuss
my hunger.
I was imprisoned; and you quietly crept off to your chapel and
prayed for my release.
I was naked; and in your mind you debated the morality of my
appearance.
I was sick; and you knelt and thanked God for your health.
I was homeless; and you preached to me of the spiritual shelter
of the love of God.
I was lonely; and you left me alone to pray for me.
You seem so holy, so close to God. But I am still hungry;
and lonely; and cold.*

I wonder sometimes just why we treat some members of our society as outcasts. Is it because they offend our sense of what is right? Is it that they are quite simply offensive? Or is it because they make us feel guilty? Is it because we feel ashamed of what we have allowed them to become? We have all of us a pre-conceived notion of what makes someone "acceptable" to society; anyone failing to conform to that "ideal" deserves no more than rejection. Psychologists and sociologists tell us of what are known to them as in-groups and out-groups: we accept quite willingly members of the first – indeed we count ourselves such members – while ignoring or, worse, taunting and persecuting members of the second. But herein lies one of the major dilemmas facing us today.

We are living in a very troubled world, and in a very troubled country. We are in this country fortunate: we are wealthy, healthy beyond the imaginations of people living no more than a century ago, and we are well able to help those less fortunate than ourselves, whether our own countrymen or refugees from elsewhere, across the world. And many do. The financial results of the Christian Aid campaigns, of countless charities large and small, the incredible reactions to the natural disasters which seem to hit us ever more frequently, are testament to that open-hearted generosity.

But that cannot and must not blind us to the fact that we are not all so munificent: that charitableness is often quite selective, even among those of us who count ourselves generous; while among those who do not give the antagonism is often quite vicious. We live in a sadly heartless time, and we have less and less space in our consciences for those worse off than ourselves, and even less will to give, so that these unfortunates might have a better life.

We live, too, in a sadly deceitful world, where too many otherwise quite healthy people are quite happy to sponge off the goodwill of the rest of us. It may be that this is one of the root causes of that antagonism, for we are none of us happy to be taken advantage of in such a callous way. However that should not obscure the fact that there are many genuinely in need: the homeless in London streets; children who have left home to escape violence and abuse; refugees who are desperate to start a new life in comparative security. Many of our charities have become adept in discriminating between the spurious and the truly genuine cases; we need perhaps to follow their example, and not so blithely reject those in need simply because they do not measure up to our high, and often quite invalid, standards.

If we seek guidance on this vexed question, we should perhaps go back to the Gospels: St Matthew (25: 34-46) has it all in a nutshell.

Points to Ponder

What sort of "outcasts" do you respond to positively?
And which negatively?
What criteria do you use to make the distinction?

ON SOCIETY

A strong society – a strong community – can tolerate a small minority of weak or feckless people whilst the majority is strong and reliable. It can tolerate a handful of sick and disabled if the majority is fit and healthy. It can tolerate a few lazy spongers if the majority is prepared to work hard. It can tolerate a few dishonest people if the majority is to be trusted. It can tolerate a small number of law-breakers if the majority is law-abiding. It can even tolerate a few evil people if the majority is in the old sense of the word "good".

Mrs Thatcher, as she was then, upset a great many people when she said: "There is no such thing as society". I think that she was at least in part wrong; but she went on to say, and that is what all her enemies have conveniently ignored: "There are individuals and there are families". The only political arrangements which have decried the individual or the family have been Communist or Fascist. Most right-thinking people now accept that the health of society depends heavily on the health of the individual and of the family. Society is in effect simply the sum total of all the individuals and families living within it; but that society cannot work if those individuals try to exercise too much personal freedom. Freedom is now the "in thing": anything which interferes with one's freedom of action is by definition wrong – even evil. That is nonsense. From time immemorial philosophers and politicians have had again and again to re-establish the correct balance between the extremes: on the one hand the society where no-one pays allegiance to the duties and obligations which we owe to each other; and on the other the society which is so strictly regimented that individuals have no scope for their individuality. That balance will not always be constant.

In the last two hundred years or so in this country we made considerable progress in ridding ourselves of those weak, sick, feckless, criminal minorities; and our society grew strong. In the last few years, however, we have begun to slip, and slip badly. Those small minorities have begun to grow again, encouraged by the idea of rights over obligations, privileges over duties. If one is to believe the reports, they are growing at such a rate as to threaten all the achievements of the past two centuries;

and many people fear for the well-being of our society. The papers are full every week, every day, of stories of mindless violence, theft, physical abuse and worse: make your own selection.

Let me bring it a little nearer home. Many have been the victims of petty or not-so-petty theft; or have lost privileges because of the selfishness of others; or have had property or surroundings vandalised. A few have been the victims of unprovoked violence. I have heard stories where a few very young children will provoke a set-to that can be exploited by older and tougher louts looking for a fight. Is this really where our civilisation is leading us? Two thousand years ago Seneca wrote: "Where there is not modesty, nor regard for law, nor religion, reverence, good faith, the kingdom is insecure". Someone else wrote: "When liberty destroys order, the hunger for order will destroy liberty". Society is like a clock: a well-running society is one where one hardly notices its running, or its motive power. But a clock begins to seize up when grit gets into the mechanism. In society the weak, the feckless, the spongers, the invalids, the crooks, all provide the specks of grit. Too many of them, and the clock simply stops. In Dunblane, a few years ago; in Marlborough before that; over Lockerbie; any number of incidents in Northern Ireland: all these have been caused by a man or men who – whatever their reasons or motives – quite suddenly proved to be a much larger lump of grit than society could tolerate.

That the evil will always be with us – like the poor – is a truism. But many of us wish only to live in peace, with ourselves and with our neighbours. Only an inflated sense of injustice, or of one's rights, coupled with the loss of a sense of obligation, duty, responsibility even compassion to our fellows, stands in the way.

Points to Ponder

What do you understand by the word "society"?
Where do you see the balance between the individual and society?
Are you happy with the balance as it is here in our society? If not, how would you want to see it shifted?

ON ST ANDREW

Of all the patron saints of the United Kingdom, the best known, because he was also one of Christ's Apostles, is also the one about whom we really know the least. Andrew, and his brother Simon Peter, the Bible tells us, were the first Apostles to be called as they walked the shores of Lake Galilee. He seems also to have been one of the "inner group" of disciples: he seems to have taken the lead, especially in that miracle known as the feeding of the five thousand, when Jesus fed a huge throng from the offerings of five loaves and two fishes from a young boy. Some commentators think that Andrew was also the "other disciple whom Jesus loved" referred to at the end of St John's Gospel, when Peter runs to the opened sepulchre where Jesus had been buried. Beyond that all is speculation, for there is very little in the way of historical evidence or documentary proof to help us. It is likely that Andrew went on to be a leading light in the infant Church; that he preached and taught, until the authorities caught up with him and tradition has it that he was crucified, at a place called Patras, on an X-shaped cross. Hence the saltire which is the Scottish flag of today.

Perhaps all that is fairly unimportant. In olden times people looked to the saints and others to be their intercessors with God – their patrons, if you like. Individuals and nations alike looked for protection from their patrons, prayed to them for help in times of danger or difficulty; or for success in battle or in negotiations. Some may decry such devotion; but in many cases such faith seems to have worked minor miracles, or perhaps the mere belief that the saint's help and protection was forthcoming was enough to give those who prayed the strength to do what was necessary. Andrew seems to have been a popular saint for this purpose: he was adopted by Scotland, and also by Russia and by Greece. Perhaps not surprisingly he was also the saint adopted by fishermen and sailors; and perhaps more inexplicably by spinsters. Saints' days in the mediaeval calendar were the opportunity for those groups to invoke their protection for the coming year.

Saints perform another even more useful function: they hold up to us a criterion of what we could be if we were to follow their example. It is a given of the Christian faith that there was but one man who was perfect, and that all other human beings will fail to reach the high standard that Jesus set us. What is so often overlooked is that many people strove, and continue to strive, to reach that standard, even though they were, and are, doomed to failure. The rest of us now regard them as saints, forgetting that within each one of us there is enough of the divine spark to help us rise to become, if not saints, then at least better human beings than might otherwise be the case. That is a message that we can remember, not just today, but on every day of the year.

Points to Ponder

Do saints provide us with a valuable example?
Is the concept of sainthood now outdated and irrelevant?
Are we all capable to some degree of "sainthood"?

ON ST DAVID

In common with at least Saint Andrew and Saint George, we know very little about Saint David, or Dewi, the patron saint of Wales, whose day we celebrate on March 1st. Of the four patron saints in these islands, David was at least Welsh; none of the others originated in the country which holds them as patrons. He was born at the beginning of the sixth century but we do not know exactly when. Tradition has it that he was the son of a princely family; that he was sent to France to study under Paulinus, who later became the first Archbishop of York; and that he returned to Wales, where he founded twelve monasteries which maintained a very austere code of conduct. He himself was consecrated bishop in Jerusalem, and returned to Menevia, a town which later became known as St David's, and his cathedral still stands there.

In common with so many "saints", David seems to have been a difficult and very demanding character. It must perhaps be borne in mind that only those who are prepared to make thundering nuisances of themselves actually achieve anything. We are perhaps too used to that concept of "sainthood" which sees only a meek submissiveness, and which people too often use to deride all the other messages of Christianity. Some certainly were meek in that way; some certainly saw their path to salvation lying in a passive acceptance of everything that life could throw at them; some certainly believed that any form of active resistance to force or evil was as evil as the prime cause. All of which seems to stem from a misinterpretation of Jesus' message as we have it in the Gospels. Yes, Jesus did not resist those who sought to capture, convict and finally kill him. But no, Jesus was no meek or submissive person: he actively challenged those whose actions he saw as evil: he threw out the moneylenders and merchants from the Temple; he threw down the gauntlet to the Pharisees, showing how their narrow and uncharitable interpretation of the Law was an insult to true religion; and he pointed up the strong contrast between those who ostentatiously showed their religion and those who simply tried to live a good life. It was that example which inspired the true saints, those who had a vision, and who were prepared to be quite cantankerous in their pursuit of that vision.

However it is not simple cantankerousness which makes a saint; if it were, there would be many more around. We recognise saints by the worthiness and righteousness of their cause; those who have the task of canonisation are unbelievably rigorous in finding whether candidates for sainthood actually measure up. Saints' contemporaries are quite unreliable in making such judgments and we need only look at those first saints, and the way in which they were regarded by the authorities of their age. This is also true of the vast majority of those of following ages. Probably none of those whom we now call saints considered themselves in that light. We too have no right to term ourselves saints, simply because we think we are. All we can do is to try to live up to the example left us by the saints – to "live the good life"; and leave the judgment to others.

Points to Ponder

Do saints provide us with a valuable example?
Is the concept of sainthood now outdated and irrelevant?
Are we all capable to some degree of "sainthood"?

ON ST GEORGE

Aboy once came to me to ask whether he might be moved from his present French set, because he "could not get on with the teacher". In normal circumstances I refused such requests: it is a part of the process of growing up that we learn to live with other people, especially those who are not easy to get on with. In this case there were some extenuating circumstances; and so I allowed him to move. A few weeks later the boy was back: he could not tolerate the new teacher either. In this case I refused, telling the boy that perhaps he was the one who needed to sort himself out. He accepted – he had to – but not without vociferous complaint: why after all should *he* be the one to change?

At university one of the texts I read was a French novel, about a man who set out with high hopes, but who found himself in all sorts of troubles from which he could not extricate himself. He develops in the course of the novel into one who constantly blames the world around him for his troubles; he too could see no reason to look within himself for the solution to his problems. The novel finally ends quite tragically, when the "hero" sees no honourable way out of his predicament, and commits suicide. In the preface to the novel the author had this to say: "Circumstances are of little importance; character is all. In vain do we break with the material world, with other people; we cannot break with ourselves. We change our situation, but we bring into each new situation the torments we hoped to leave behind; and as we cannot change by our moving, we find only that we have added remorse to our regrets, faults to our sufferings".

One of those rhetorical questions about personality is: "Can the leopard change his spots?" I believe, indeed I know, that he can: so often have I seen pupils suddenly come to realise that their way of life hitherto has been unsatisfactory, and that a drastic change is called for. Often perhaps that is triggered simply by the process of growing up; but very occasionally there seems to have been some inner trigger, some awakening to the truth that change is not only necessary, but possible. Our character, our personality, our behaviour are things over which we do have some small control, more so than over our physical appearance or our mental powers. Often that change is difficult to maintain: the road back to virtue is always hard; but I have been impressed by those who have stuck to the task, and can sympathise with those who need our help when they fall by the wayside.

Once, long ago, during the time of the Roman Empire, there was in a province called Cappadocia – what is now called Turkey – a soldier. We know very little about him save what is related in the legend; but he was probably quite typical, behaving like the hard man, given to drinking, given to swearing, fond of the women – in other words just an ordinary sinner like the rest of us. Just once in his life he performed a deed to show that he was more than that, when he offered himself as a sacrifice in place of a young woman condemned to die for the horrible crime of being a Christian. His name was George; and we commemorate him on, 23rd April, as the patron saint of England. We do not need to take on board all the myths and legends about him, although the story of his slaying the dragon to rescue a young woman holds a truth which is quite clear. What we do need to understand is that we *can* change – for the better, whether it be by reacting to such external circumstances or in response to an inner voice.

Points to Ponder

Do saints provide us with a valuable example?
Is the concept of sainthood now outdated and irrelevant?
Are we all capable to some degree of "sainthood"?
Can people change their spots?

ON ST PATRICK

Of the four patron saints within the United Kingdom, Patrick is the one whom we perhaps know best, and whose life is less hedged about by legend. Even so, there are gaps in our knowledge; but it is a fair assumption that he was born in the fifth century in Wales, although some people think that he might have been born in France; that he was the son of a Romano-British man, a Christian called Calpurnius; and that he was captured by pirates and taken to Ireland, where he stayed for six years as a slave before managing to escape. It is thought that he then studied in France to become a monk, and that he was then sent back to Ireland as a missionary.

Quite recently I read a book by Thomas Cahill, an American publisher, writer and historian, entitled *How the Irish saved Civilisation*. In it he argues that, just at the moment when Europe was collapsing into the Dark Ages, with all manner of knowledge being consigned to the fires because it was not authentically "Christian", scholars from all parts of the old Roman Empire were taking refuge in Ireland, and continuing their studies away from the persecution, the perils and the dangers from the new Vandals. These scholars helped to perpetuate this knowledge, by copying the texts for wider circulation, and by preaching a rather more tolerant message than was the norm in Europe. Cahill goes on to argue that if this more laid-back approach had been allowed to prevail, the history of Europe in the coming centuries would have been vastly different.

And this is where we come back to Patrick. That his early life was hard and full of danger seems quite clear. Such experiences can turn one either way: they can make the victim embittered and determined on revenge and retribution; or they can be positive, in that the victim tries to ensure that no-one else should suffer in the same way. Patrick seems to have fallen into the latter category. The view of Thomas Cahill is that Patrick was of just the right temperament to harness the old virtues of his pagan Celtic society with the new virtues of Christianity; and that this led eventually to a much more open and tolerant way of life. Legend has it that Patrick felt summoned in a dream to return to Ireland to convert the "heathen" to Christianity: he seems to have been able to use his knowledge of the customs of the island to win over the clan chieftains, and thence their followers. But he seems also to have been quite outspoken when the occasion demanded and some felt that he regarded martyrdom as a great virtue, and then set out to court it. He is known to have written in very strong terms to one Coroticus, a British chieftain who had taken a group of Irish Christians hostage, and who was treating them abominably. He is known to have used the shamrock, the three-leaved clover, to illustrate the message of the Trinity to his converts; but whether there is any truth in the legend that he rid the island of Ireland of snakes is unknowable. One thing is certain: that he managed to identify with the Irish of his time; and that sense of identity is now very strong in reverse, with everyone of Irish descent, across the world, treating him with immense deference. The 17th March is his feast day and is therefore an occasion for a vivid display of Irish-ism.

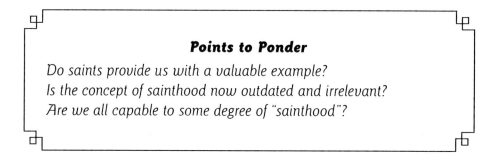

Points to Ponder

Do saints provide us with a valuable example?
Is the concept of sainthood now outdated and irrelevant?
Are we all capable to some degree of "sainthood"?

Book to Read:

Thomas Cahill – How the Irish Saved Civilisation

ON TEACHING AND LEARNING

I sometimes think that Sisyphus, the man condemned by the gods to push a boulder up a cliff, only to have it thrown down again so that he could repeat the process, must have been a teacher. In the same way teachers collect new batches of little boulders at the start of each new school year – to add to the collections which have been already assembled, and then start the job of pushing them up the hill of knowledge for the next five, six, seven years. Perhaps the only difference is that the boulders get bigger and heavier as the years pass.

As we grow older, the idea that we never stop learning becomes more acceptable. Young people also seem to be able to accept, with their growing maturity, that old fogeys do actually know a thing or two. Mark Twain is quoted as saying that when he was eighteen he thought his father a fool; when he reached twentyone he was surprised to see how much his father had learned in three years.

But what is teaching? What is learning? Galileo once said: "You cannot teach a man anything; you can only help him to find it within himself". Another less well-known man, Velen Vanderlik, a professor of the university at Vancouver, said something similar. When he retired his students threw a dinner in his honour; and during his retirement speech he said that he had never taught anyone anything:

"You said, we taught you so many things. Did we? Nobody has ever taught anybody anything. We just helped you to learn. It was your work, and after you come through this gate into life it will be also your responsibility..... We tried to teach you more than we knew, we taught you to think and to understand. To be able to find out and to think out something which no-one knows today..... We tried to plant in your hearts the seed of "amor sciendi" – the quest for knowledge, the desire to know for the sake of knowing alone. When Malory, the New Zealander, was asked why he attempted to climb Mount Everest, he said simply: "Because it is there". If anybody asks you why did you learn this, or other things, tell him: "Because I wanted to know".

Once you have got used to that idea, becoming the horse which comes willingly to water *and* is happy to drink from it, then you become an active partner in your development. Oliver Wendell Holmes said once: "The human mind, once stretched to a new idea, never goes back to its original dimensions".

There are three things that come to mind. The first is the Parable of the Talents, which I find cropping up quite often in my talks; it is a very rich story, full of hidden depths. All too often young people leave school to join the wide world which is so full of opportunity, without ever having discovered their own abilities or preferences. Good schools offer opportunities, to explore what is available, whether it be in sport, or in academic pursuits, or in social or free-time activities. How will pupils make their contribution to society, if they have never taken the trouble to discover what they are good at, the things that they like doing? And perhaps even more important, what they dislike, or the things for which they have no talent. Each year as pupils left I pondered on whether any would leave without giving these matters some thought?

The second is perhaps the psychological basis of learning theory, which need not worry us in any detail. In more general terms: in the words of a notorious school report – "They say that we learn from our mistakes; this child must know an awful lot by now". We do not learn by a painless process of osmosis: we learn by hard work, by worrying at tasks, even by failing a bit; we learn by trial and error, we learn by example, by imitation, by precept. Teachers have a duty to pass on what has been decried as "high culture" – the best that our civilisation has to offer; we have a duty to pass on the values which make us civilised; we have a duty to pass on the accumulated wisdom of the years, so that you have no need to keep on "re-inventing the wheel", as it is called. Those duties have been much derided: in modern eyes what is important is the here and now; there is no need to hark back to a bygone and therefore no longer relevant era; everyone has to work out their own ethical framework, with no lip-service even to those ethical considerations which have been shown to work so effectively.

The last is the need for that firm ethical framework for our learning – for ethics embody what is true and right for all generations. In former days the priests, of whatever persuasion, tried to give a lead. Moses brought down from the mountain just ten Commandments; by the time of Christ those ten had spawned a mass of thousands of dogmatic statements about man's relationships, with man and with God. Christ himself simplified that mass to just two: love God, love your neighbour. That so many people now reject the authority of priests does not mean that they can with impunity reject their precepts. If you can fit all you learn into that framework, not much else can go very wrong.

Never forget that learning is for life. To quote another writer: "The things you learn in maturity aren't simple things such as acquiring information and skills. You learn not to engage in self-destructive behaviour. You learn not to burn up energy in anxiety. You discover how to manage stress. You learn that self-pity and resentment are among the most toxic of drugs. You find that the world loves talent, but rewards character. You come to understand that most people are neither for you nor against you; they are thinking about themselves. You learn that no matter how hard you try to please, some people in this world are not going to love you – a lesson that is at first troubling and then really quite relaxing".

Points to Ponder

Are you an active, or a passive learner? Do you take pleasure in taking part in a lesson – or in trying to avoid the teacher's attention? Do you see learning as "cool"?
Do you enjoy more a lesson in which you have been actively engaged, or one in which you have simply listened to the teacher?

ON THE HUMAN PARADOX

Some of you might perhaps know the story of Spartacus, the escaped slave who in ancient Roman times held the Imperial power at bay for a time, fighting for more humane treatment for the likes of himself, before being captured and executed. One of the novels written round the story, by Arthur Koestler, has this said by one of his characters, who sees that Spartacus is having to achieve his goals of freedom, peace and justice by the same cruel and inhumane methods as the Romans themselves:

"God created the world in five days, and He was in too much of a hurry. Many things went wrong in all his hurry, and when he arrived at the making of man on the sixth day, he was irritable and tired perhaps, and he burdened man with curses. But the worst curse of all is that he must tread the evil road for the sake of the good and right, that he must make detours and walk crookedly so that he may reach the straight goal."

Life is full of such paradoxes. Perhaps it is in politics that the results of certain actions are often the opposite of those sought – the law of unintended consequences. I have seen it operate in the ways in which our leaders, from the best intentions, try to make life better, but in ways which are almost bound to make life worse for all. Aristotle summed it up when he said: "The worst form of inequality is to try to make unequal things equal". Abraham Lincoln had the same idea when he pointed out that one does not improve the lot of the weak or helpless by damaging those who are better placed.

But it happens also in school. Teachers who act with the best of humanitarian principles, who act with friendliness, sympathy and understanding, may be regarded as "friends", but they are also taken advantage of in what is wrongly seen as their weakness; and so they fail to achieve the results which their effort and example seek. Those who see good results are all too often those who treat others like dirt, trampling on finer feelings, administering the figurative kick in the teeth. What a pity.

I still believe and hope that the civilised, compassionate, humane way to treat others is the best way. In my experience it takes a good deal longer; but at least occasionally it has a longer-lasting effect. That said, I am interested in seeing results, especially with young people, in seeing them develop into worthy and more effective characters; and when I see that kindness is interpreted as weakness, in that it doesn't produce those effects; and that bloody-mindedness is strength, in that it does, I must ask myself whether I have not after all this time been mistaken. Think about it: co-operation with others is not the end of the world – we do after all have a common enemy – ignorance; it is no slur on growing independence to admit that your elders are sometimes your betters. Part of a teacher's job is to help pupils to know themselves: to recognise the good and to learn to develop it and to build on it; to recognise the darker side and to learn to restrict and inhibit it. I was always saddened when I heard complaints of continued discourtesy to others, of foul language, of laxity in attitudes to work and to the necessary disciplines and routines of school life. But I was equally cheered to hear the reverse, to know that strivings towards responsibility, maturity and at-one-ness with the world were beginning to bear fruit.

Points to Ponder

Do you like the teachers you respect?
Do you respect the teachers you like?
Can you in fact do both – like and respect?
Which comes first – the liking, or the respect?
Should either quality colour the way you behave towards them?

ON THE LAW

The humanbeing is a gregarious animal – living in herds, societies, clans. And because he (or she) is not a solitary animal, he has to surrender some of his freedom of action if he is to live in peace and harmony with others. If life is to be tolerable for all, all must accept that an insistence on their rights has to be curtailed in some degree. The balance between one's rights and one's responsibilities is a delicate one, and probably needs to be re-established with each generation. That is why we need laws. Too much freedom in one direction will lead to a breakdown in order, and the demand for a return to order may well destroy that freedom. If we can willingly accept such restraints as are necessary for us all to enjoy our rights, life will be much more pleasant for all. I remember a headmaster long ago saying that he would love to have a school without rules: not of course for the sheer anarchy which would inevitably result, but simply because every pupil – *every* pupil – would know what was expected, and would behave accordingly.

Most schools have a code of rules which, for the most part, give guidance on relationships with each other. It is expected that those rules will be adhered to, for the comfort and safety of all. If the rules are broken then there will be punishment more or less severely, according to the gravity of the offence. As in school, so in the world at large. A good government, one with self-confidence and the confidence of its electors, will enact those laws which are wanted and needed, and more importantly will enforce them. Similarly, it will not enact laws which run contrary to the will of the people, for in the end, at least in our tradition, governments act with the consent of the people.

Of late there has been a tendency for the law to fall into disrepute: there are too many laws which are not approved by the people, while many laws are not enforced with sufficient authority. There has been a disapproval of people taking "the law into their own hands", although, again in our tradition, that is exactly where the law should be. That is why we have lay juries and lay magistrates – to underline the way in which the law is what the people say it is; and the way in which there is an open link between the law and the people. We have established what we call the rule of law simply because individuals should not be allowed to interpret the law in any way they wish; but that it should be seen to be fair, consistent and impartial and slightly detached from the immediacy of the crime or offence. Indeed, the mediaeval Icelanders worked on this very precept: their Parliament, the Althing, was set up to try to establish that *all* people were subject to the same code of law, and to enforce that law quite disinterestedly.

In less civilised times, those who broke the law continuously were termed outlaws. Such people were no longer considered to be bound by the law of the land – a nice freedom, perhaps. But they were also denied the protection of the law; the consequence was that their lives were not the glamorous idyll of the Wild West or of Robin Hood, but were, in Hobbes's words: "solitary, poor, nasty, brutish and short". There is a telling episode in Robert Bolt's play *A Man for all Seasons*, when Thomas More is talking to his son-in-law. The latter has boasted that he would cut down every law in the land if it enabled him to reach the Devil. Thomas challenges him on this, asking him where he will turn for his own protection when the Devil finally rounds on him. In like vein we must these days ask where those who have destroyed the law by their contempt and arrogance will turn for protection from those who wish only to be left to live in peace and security and harmony.

Points to Ponder

The law can tell us how to behave; can it make us good?
Is the law being applied vigorously enough?
Can the average citizen really now rely on the
protection of the law?
Is it possible to reinvigorate the rule of law?

Books to Read:

Robert Bolt: *A Man for all Seasons*

ON THE LESSONS OF HISTORY

Ours is a very rich history; and scarcely a year passes without there being some anniversary of some historical event which we would do well to mark. Some of these have to do with our development as a nation such as the Magna Carta, the Civil War, the Bill of Rights. Others have to do with our survival as a nation – Trafalgar, Remembrance Day, the Battle of Britain. At other times we remember, with affection, or gratitude, or respect, the individuals who have helped to shape those events.

To pick an example at random: 1989 was a vintage year for anniversaries. The Mutiny on the Bounty was the subject of an impressive exhibition at Greenwich; the Bill of Rights was likewise celebrated in the Banqueting Hall in Whitehall; the French Revolution had the French nation in festive mood all year, incidentally incorporating the centenary of the Eiffel Tower. The one which perhaps stood out that year, for remembering rather than perhaps for celebrating, was the fiftieth anniversary of the outbreak of the Second World War. For several years after, we were being reminded of the half-century which had passed since this campaign, that battle, some other significant event had taken place. And now we approach the seventieth anniversary.

Why was that war fought? It is first perhaps as well to remind ourselves that a knowledge of history is important if we are to avoid repeating past errors, and to learn what might be useful lessons. The more meaningful developments in our history have often come about as challenges to the legitimacy of the existing systems of government. Jesus told His tormentors that they should render unto Caesar what was Caesar's – and the oft-forgotten addition that they should render unto God what was God's. The Holy Roman Emperors claimed their legitimacy from God through the Pope. Charles I and Louis XIV claimed the divine right of kings. But in so many cases there were brave souls who voiced their doubts: Sir Thomas More challenged Henry VIII; Oliver Cromwell challenged Charles I; many thinkers challenged Louis XIV. The results, often achieved at considerable cost in time, money and even blood, were some form of what is now known as constitutional government: our own Bill of Rights, the Rights of Man in France; the US Constitution; the Grundgesetz in Germany.

All these developments presupposed that governments can, and will try to, act against the best interests of those they are elected to serve; and that they therefore need to be kept within bounds.

When such clashes occur, the people in charge will do their utmost to hold on to power. Peterloo in 1819; the year of revolutions in 1848; the Russian Revolution in 1917; in China, in Tiananmen Square – all serve to remind us that power, and who wields it, is important. As Lord Acton said, all power corrupts; absolute power corrupts absolutely and a good example of this was the Ceausescus in Romania! So it was in 1939. I recently read a book about the Resistance, within Germany, to the rise of Nazism. Such resistance, to what had been legally brought into force, but which was nonetheless morally and ethically wrong, required a strength of purpose, a stamina which perhaps we have lost in the comparatively soft days since the war ended.

We still need to resist what is wrong, or evil, or just plain stupid. At a time when so many countries across the world are undergoing change in their systems of government – violent, or gradual; overt, or by stealth – we need clarity of vision and perseverance to overcome the apathy and inertia on which the "bosses" rely. Such people do not like opposition, even if the ideas which such tension produces are demonstrably better; they do not like challenge, especially if it forces them to change their minds; they do not like uncertainty, all the more so if they have to admit that they may have been wrong.

There are two quotations which I would like you to bear in mind. I do not know the source of the first: "The worst service that the Devil can do us is to persuade us that he does not exist". The second is from Edmund Burke: "All that is required for the triumph of evil is that good men should do nothing".

Points to Ponder

Does the present teaching of history trivialise our past?
Can we still learn from our past! If so, what lessons should we draw?
Should we take more pride in our history?
Or should we always be ashamed of the actions of our forbears?

ON THE NEW YEAR

I would like to start with three quotations. The first is by Minnie Louise Haskins, and was used by King George VI in one of his Christmas addresses:

> "And I said to the man who stood at the gate of the year: "Give me a light, that I may tread safely into the unknown". And he replied: "Go out into the darkness and put your hand into the hand of God. That shall be to you better than light and safer than a known way"."

The second is from Charles Lamb:

> "Every first of January that we arrive at is an imaginary milestone on the turnpike track of human life: at once a resting place for thought and meditation, and a starting point for fresh exertion in the performance of our journey. The man who does not at least propose to himself to be better this year than he was last, must be either very good or very bad indeed."

The third is by Fra Giovanni, and dates from 1513:

> "Life is so full of meaning and purpose, so full of beauty beneath its cover, that you find that the earth only cloaks your heaven. Courage, then, to claim it – that is all. But courage you have, the knowledge that we are pilgrims together through unknown territory. And so I greet you, not quite as the world does but with profound esteem and with the prayer that for you, now and always, the day breaks and the shadows flee."

Time is one of our most precious commodities: like any other resource we should beware of wasting it. *Pace* Charles Lamb, we need every so often to stop, to take stock and especially now, for there is something quite mystic about the New Year, with its promise of better things to come. Not for nothing is the turn of the year the occasion for revelry. So stop and take stock. What happened last year that you regretted, or that you felt could have been done better? What can you do better this year; what should you try not to do; what new things can you undertake; how, in short, can you improve your lot, your contribution to the common weal? I would not wish to be misunderstood: I am talking not just, or even mainly, about academic performance; but about personal development – as individual men and women. As a teacher several times in the course of the year I was encouraged by the way in which a pupil suddenly awoke to the realisation that it was not too late; and that no matter that the road might be long and rough, taking a particular turning was the right, proper and worthwhile thing to do.

All of us have another New Year ahead of us, to do with as we choose. Some things are pre-ordained, and therefore unavoidable. But for the most part the future *is* the unknown, the darkness: how we cope will depend very largely on the sort of critical appraisal we make of the past, the sort of "resolution" we now show, the sort of faith we can muster to face that future. I wish you well!

Points to Ponder

Do you see the New Year as a time for renewal?
What would you need to change about your own life?
What new developments would you like to undertake?

ON TIME

We often need to think hard about the resources that we have at our disposal. In the words of a wise man, all the world's resources do not belong to us – we are no more than their trustees, and we in effect borrow them from our children. Back in the Sixties one of the movements of the Christian Church was known as Christian Stewardship: again the idea that we held our resources in trust, to use not only, and certainly not primarily, for our own benefit, but for all those who might have need of them.

There is one resource in particular that is freely available to us all, and that is time. Arnold Bennett once wrote an essay, to the effect that no matter how we wasted or misused our time, we were every morning granted another twenty-four hours to do with as we wished. When I was rather younger I seized upon that idea with some enthusiasm, for I found it quite comforting. With advancing years I am no longer sure that it is a valid idea. The message from a number of sources is the same, from Horace to Herrick: Carpe diem; the wise and the foolish virgins; "Gather ye rosebuds while ye may"; "Let us eat, drink and be merry, for tomorrow we die". There is also the question of habit: if we once become used to the idea of wasting time, we may never be able, as addicts find it impossible to break their addiction, to break back to a more useful disposition of our time.

Throughout life there are always hurdles to tackle – time-dictated obstacles to a quiet life: examinations, university life, finding a job. In my experience none of these are set in stone; you can, if you miss the chance, try again later; there will always be further windows of opportunity. But it is always extremely difficult to do something later in life when you have perhaps lost the requisite skills and habits. Even making those decisions which are forced upon you need not necessarily be final or irrevocable; nevertheless you will find it easier to make those decisions at the appropriate moment. We will each of us enjoy rather easier and more pleasant lives by accepting that the time of each one of us is precious, and that the waste of time, like the waste of any other resource, is to be avoided.

There is another aspect of the question that I would like to commend to you. Albert Schweitzer once wrote that all of us owe it to our fellow humans to set aside time – unpaid, unrewarded, unrecognised if need be – for those who need our help. One of the things that has impressed me about the schools where I worked is that all of them felt that effort for others was important, and there were charity collections and the like. I noticed also that older pupils were already giving of their time and talents to help the less fortunate, working, for example, in hospitals, nurseries, or special schools. When we are young we are at the time of life when taking is important: taking from parents, taking from teachers, or from youth leaders. But as we mature we have to begin to turn our thoughts towards the notion of putting back something of what we have taken – not necessarily to those from whom it has been taken, but to others who in their turn will take and then give.

Points to Ponder

How well do we organise our time?
Are all our activities useful or positive or productive?
Do we make time for ourselves alone, or also for others?
At the same time, do we give ourselves time to "sit and stare"?

ON TOLERANCE I

The Age of Enlightenment – the eighteenth century – was a time of massive intellectual ferment. There was a veritable explosion of knowledge; incidentally putting paid to the marvellous concept of the universal man, the man who could master all that there was to know. There was a buzz of new ideas, philosophic, scientific and artistic. Even with all this activity, there were still those with the optimistic view that knowledge should be accessible to all; and so the first encyclopaedias were born.

As with all revolutions, there were the forces of reaction to be reckoned with. In France these took the form of the monarchy and the Church; and the intolerance which these two institutions showed led men like Voltaire to seek refuge in rather more tolerant countries, of which England at the time was the leader. Voltaire was the victim of some quite vicious persecution; some of it perhaps well-deserved, for he was by all accounts quite an awkward character. But it was he who preached the code of tolerance; he who first asserted the right to hold an opinion even if others found that opinion inconvenient or unacceptable. He wrote: "I do not agree with what you are saying; but I will defend to the death your right to say it".

Today we seem in some danger of slipping back into those uncomfortable reactionary times. Some years ago three history teachers from very different backgrounds were all sacked for daring to teach their subject in ways considered to be contrary to received wisdom. They may well have been just such cussed and pigheaded individuals as Voltaire; but they should still have been allowed at least to argue their case. More recently there has been the case of Salman Rushdie: whatever one may think of his novels, whatever may have been the rights and wrongs of his case (and I think that he was wrong not to accept that his writings gave serious offence) no reasonable person could condone the idea that he should be executed for his views. Another case concerns a school where I was for several years a governor. At the time the local authority put forward a plan to sell the school so that it could be converted into a City Technical College. The governors, the teachers and almost all the local population were dead set against the idea; but it was some time before the local authority could be persuaded to back down. There is also the novel *The Fountainhead*, which is the story of an architect whose ideas were far too original for the establishment, which tried to destroy him.

All these cases have in common the individual's right to think and say what is important to him. We have, quite rightly, laws which prevent us from saying things which are defamatory, or which could incite violence. All these cases have in common the absence of any attempt to reason with the opposition; instead opposition is to be bullied into silence. Now we must all admit that such a reaction is much easier; but in the long run it is quite useless. To convince people by reason is ultimately much better, for they will then be with you in what you are trying to do, rather than still against you.

Despite the attitude of some people, most teachers question not opinions, but the way in which these are sometimes expressed. I believe that everyone has the right to their own opinions; and they have the right to express them; they also have the right to expect others to listen – though not necessarily to take any notice. For anyone wishing to express an opinion there are however three parallel duties: to know what they are talking about; to be ready to accept that they might *not* know what they are talking about; and above all to be courteous and correct in dealings with others. There is an old French proverb: "Si la jeunesse savait; si la vieillesse pouvait". That should perhaps be at the back of our minds when we think about this: older people have the benefit of experience, and it is hoped, wisdom; but the young need to supply the energy and enthusiasm which must be balanced with the lack of experience, but which the older people may have lost. To ignore that need is to prolong what is in my view foolishly termed the generation gap. Society is what people of older generations have made of it; and I cannot claim any particular pride in their achievements. The young owe it to themselves to sort out where previous generations went wrong; then go out and do better. *That* is tolerance.

Points to Ponder

Can we legislate for tolerance? Does the existence of laws to prevent intolerance actually encourage it? How can we inculcate tolerance of others – especially those of whom we actively disapprove?
Have we done enough to explore the existence of common ground between apparently irreconcilable groups?

ON TOLERANCE II

A trainee teacher under my mentorship once asked me if she might put out a questionnaire about the ways in which religion, and more specifically Christianity, was fostered within the school. I have to say that the school concerned was, of all the schools where I have worked or which I have seen in action, probably the most tolerant in this respect. I found out from that survey that a number of the pupils in the school had been teased and even bullied on account of their religious beliefs. I know also that the average teenager – boys possibly more so than girls – find it hard to acknowledge any form of religious beliefs to their peers. Nevertheless it seemed to me that we were fortunate to have such a tolerant view of these matters.

We all know from our history about quarrels between different faiths: the Crusades were a case in point, but this has been reinforced by differences in the Balkans, in the Middle East, in Indonesia. I find that there is possibly less tolerance between members of the same faith than between those of different faiths. I am myself a Christian, a Free Churchman; my wife is a Catholic. Luckily we have no problems. But one needs only to look at Northern Ireland to see where the so-called practitioners of religion can indulge in quite outrageous behaviour in defence of their "beliefs". In less recent times we read of the struggles between Christian sects; between the different wings of Islam and Judaism; and the intolerance shown towards the more traditional forms by some of the weirder modern cults claiming to be Christian. I once found a quotation to the effect that there would be a great deal less evil in the world if only we would not practise evil in the name of what is good.

I would remind you of the psychologists' concept of in-groups and out-groups: the in-groups are those which we belong to, which we support, either because we believe in those groups' ideals or because we wish to be accepted by those groups. The out-groups are those we do not support, which in extreme cases we regard with fear or loathing, either real or imagined. These groups can be based on kinship; on sport (the antagonism between fans of different football teams is legendary); on politics; or religion; or race. In my experience the antipathy seems to vary in inverse proportion to one's confidence in one's own beliefs or ideals.

In the eighteenth century – the Age of Enlightenment – the great German playwright Lessing wrote a play entitled *Nathan the Wise Man*, set in the time of the Crusades. The three main protagonists are Nathan himself, a Jew; the Knight Templar, a Christian; and Saladin, the leader of the Muslim forces in Jerusalem. Lessing knew all about persecution; he even foresaw, in a chilling essay, the forces of evil which Hitler would unleash on Europe two hundred years later. But in this play there is a story related by Nathan, which has become known as the *Ringlegendchen*. A man once possessed a ring which conferred upon its wearer wisdom and a power and influence for good over other men. Tradition in the family had it that the owner would bequeath the ring to the one of his sons he adjudged most fit to wear it, the one he loved and cherished the best. The present owner had three sons, all of whom he loved equally. When his time to die drew near, he was in considerable difficulties as to whom he should leave the ring: all three were equally deserving. Finally he resolved his problem, by having two replicas made. To each son he gave a ring, and his blessing; and died.

The three sons then came together, each displaying his ring. Each naturally claimed that his ring was the genuine one; again naturally, strife broke out among them, to such an extent that they found it necessary to have recourse to the local magistrate to decide between them. The magistrate's advice was that each should go his way and live his life, with his brothers and his neighbours, as if he really did possess the real ring. Behaving as they were, they must all be wearing false rings.

The parable should be clear: if we spent a little less time and effort struggling to prove that we were the holders of the one true faith, and a little more in living the message of our faith, the world would be a much better place.

Points to Ponder

Can we legislate for tolerance? Does the existence of laws to prevent intolerance actually encourage it?

How can we inculcate tolerance of others – especially perhaps of those of whom we actively disapprove?

Have we done enough to explore the existence of common ground between apparently irreconcilable groups?

ON TRUST

In his letter to Timothy (2 Timothy 1: 12-14) Paul talks of what he has entrusted to God; and he urges Timothy to safeguard the trust which God has placed in him. The Greek word which Paul uses is one which means a deposit committed to someone's trust. In the ancient world there was no more sacred duty than the safeguarding of such a trust, and its safe return when it was claimed after due time. There was a time, in the not too distant past, when a man's word was his bond; all that was necessary was a handshake. The reputation of the City of London, as a centre for finance and insurance, was founded on this one fact – that a gentleman's word once given was unbreakable, even without documentary proof such as would be insisted upon today. Even today there are many people who still assert, some would say quite stupidly, that their word should be treated with the same respect; and the Scout movement, again perhaps unrealistically, also expects members to aim for the ideal that "A Scout's honour is to be trusted".

There is an old story that tells how sacred such a trust was considered to be. The Spartans were famous for their strict honour and honesty. A certain man of Miletus came to see Glaucus of Sparta. He said that he had heard such great reports of the Spartans' honesty that he had turned half of his possessions into money; and that he wished to deposit that money with Glaucus until he or his heirs should have need of it and claim it back. Certain symbols called tallies were given and received, which would identify the rightful claimant when the claim was made. The years passed on, the man of Miletus died, and his sons came to Sparta to see Glaucus. They produced the identifying tallies and asked for the return of the money. But Glaucus claimed that he had no recollection of ever having received money in this way. The men from Miletus went away sadly; but Glaucus went to the famous Oracle at Delphi to ask what he should do: whether he should admit the trust; or whether, as he was entitled to do, he should swear that he knew nothing about the matter – for the Greeks accepted such an oath as true.

The Oracle answered in this way: "Best for the present it were, O Glaucus, to do as thou wishest, swearing an oath to prevail and so to make a prize of the money. Swear then – for death is the lot even of those who never swear falsely. Yet the Oath God hath a son who is nameless, footless and handless. Mighty in strength he approaches vengeance and overwhelms in destruction all who belong to the race or the house of the man who is perjured. But oath-keeping men leave behind them a flourishing offspring."

Glaucus understood: the Oracle was telling him that if he was seeking for monetary profit he should deny the trust; but that such a denial would bring eternal loss. Glaucus begged the Oracle to pardon his question; but the answer was that to have tempted the God was as bad as having done the deed. He sent for the sons of the man from Miletus and restored the money. But then the story goes on: "Glaucus has at this time not a single descendant; nor is there any family known as his; root and branch has he been removed from Sparta. It is a good thing therefore when a pledge has been left with one, not even in thought to doubt restoring it." To the Greeks a trust, a deposit, was completely sacred.

Can your word be trusted in the same way?

Points to Ponder

Can the betrayal of trust ever be justified?
Is it right to break a promise, on the grounds that it "was only a verbal agreement"?
Can we justify a request to be released from a promise – as Glaucus asked the Oracle?

ON TRUTH AND FACT

When I was at school, at the height of the Cold War, the story was going the rounds about an athletics match between Russia and America. America won: the event was reported there as America winning, Russia losing. But in Russia the Russians came second, the Americans last but one. In both cases accurate reporting of the facts; but hardly a truthful representation.

More seriously: before WW2 the then Archbishop of Canterbury was on a pastoral visit to the States. When he landed at New York he was greeted by the usual press conference, during which he was asked whether he would be visiting a brothel during his stay. Naively he asked whether there really were brothels in New York. The following day the newspapers bore the headline: "Archbishop's first question: are there brothels here in New York?" Again factually correct – but misleading.

Recently scientists have made news with stories about the way in which we are destroying our planet. I came across a demonstration of the ways in which such stories are put about: a student stood outside a London Underground station and told passers-by: "A certain chemical substance is used in significant ways, and often leads to spillages and other leaks; and it regularly finds its way into rivers and into our food supply. It is a major component of acid rain. It contributes to erosion. It decreases the effectiveness of car brakes. In its vapour state it is a major greenhouse gas. It can cause excessive sweating and vomiting. Accidental inhalation can kill you. It has been found in tumours of terminally ill cancer patients. Should this chemical be controlled or even banned?" Three out of four people approached said: "Yes!"; only one in twenty disagreed. (We are not told how many asked the name of the chemical before passing judgement!) But this chemical so luridly described is – water. Again, factually correct, but highly misleading.

Some time ago Paul Johnson, the journalist, wrote about the massacre which occurred in Amsterdam on 7th May 1945. His article was accompanied by some telling photographs; but he pointed out that the photos gave only the facts of what happened; they could not tell us why or how such a bloody event came about. Nicholas Tomalin, a journalist killed during the Yom Kippur War in 1967, said just before his death that television was a marvellous medium for presenting the facts of warfare; but that only radio could enable us to discuss ways in which peace could be fostered.

I cannot help feeling that we live in an age where demonstrable provable fact is more important than truth. Witnesses in a court of law are required on oath to tell the truth, the whole truth and nothing but the truth. Often we get the first and the third; but not the second – because lawyers go out of their way to avoid eliciting such facts as may not help their case. Politicians, too, tend not to give us the truth, but instead slanted presentation of the facts. Anything which cannot be proved, in the forensic sense, is valueless and therefore to be discarded.

So it is therefore that religion is held in such low esteem. "Eminent" comedians and others tell us that, because Christianity is founded on a lie, and by that they mean the Bible, it too must be a lie. Quite right: there was no king who went away leaving vast sums of money in the hands of his servants; there was no Garden of Eden, no Adam and Eve. Because these myths are demonstrably false, we throw out the truth as well – discarding the baby with the bath-water. But these stories are "true": Jesus used His parables to illustrate the human condition, and to show how it could be bettered. The ancients used vivid stories to explain complex scientific problems to their unsophisticated audiences. A colleague of mine once said that the story of Adam and Eve is true for each one of us, as we grow up and become more aware of our physical and sexual selves. Think a little more deeply about the truths buried, sometimes now almost beyond reach, in the legends and tales which are such an integral part of our heritage; and simply feel sorry for those who are too blind, or too lacking in intelligence, to want to see the truths for themselves.

Points to Ponder

Have you ever been misled by the improper use of facts? Is it possible to enable courts of law to know the whole truth about a case?
Can we teach you how to distinguish between various levels of factual accuracy and truthfulness?

ON VIOLENCE

We are faced these days with a dilemma the like of which we have not seen since perhaps the days of the Second World War – that of violence, pre-meditated, unsolicited, indiscriminate, pitiless, and totally unjustifiable. We have a right to ask why such behaviour is to some people not only a reasonable reaction to their circumstances, but apparently the only reaction possible. Let us leave aside for the moment all the weasel words of those who really should know better; let us leave aside those who choose for their own warped reasons to blame such actions on the shortcomings of our own society; let us leave aside also the fact that violence is always – always – the most ineffective way of dealing with real or perceived grievances. Let us instead listen to what the voices of reason are trying to tell us.

There are a number of scientists, called ethologists, who study animal behaviour "in the wild" as it were – observing animals in their natural habitat. Between the wars one of the most eminent scientists in this field was a man called Sir Solly Zuckerman; and he was also a Chief Government Scientist. But he studied animals only in the confines of London Zoo – and he came to the conclusion that aggressive behaviour, backed by clear examples of violent behaviour, was an innate and inescapable feature of all animal behaviour. The ethologists, however, chief among whom was a man called Konrad Lorenz, said that the artificial environment of a zoo was no place to seek evidence about animals. Instead, they claimed, we should be looking at how they behave when left to their own devices. Lorenz went on to write several books: one is a quite beautiful account of his work, *King Solomon's Ring*. Another, more important, was *On Aggression*: in this book he suggests that assertiveness and competition are important, indeed necessary components of the human psyche, without which there can really never be any improvement in our lot. He also pointed out that there is absolutely no evidence that this needs to spill over into aggression or violence. He noted that while many animals fight among themselves, for territory, for food, for sexual partners it is only man who seems to feel the need to go further and kill his fellows. He went as far as to argue that man seemed to be locked into a sort of evolutionary cul-de-sac, where females of the species seemed to be attracted to violent males, the offspring of such unions being almost by definition equally violent. Such "progress" would inevitably lead to extinction.

To bring it back to our situation in our immediate society: is it really impossible that the minor disagreements which are an inescapable feature of our life together have to be solved only with the use of fists, or – worse – knives, guns, mob rule? Or does violence simply beget more violence, into an unending trail of vendetta, with neither side willing, or perhaps even able, to cut into the vicious circle. To come back to Lorenz, we must learn to harness the immense power of our inventiveness – with the so-called arms race producing ever more horrific ways of doing violence one to another – and to cultivate feelings of responsibility and inhibition, so that we do not wipe ourselves out by allowing our primitive instincts to rule us. Read the book – it makes fascinating, and for our period in history very timely reading.

NOTES: As far as I know no psychologists have answered properly the question: Is violence unavoidable? We have seen lately attempts to resolve the problem by means of laws; but laws are useless unless we make some attempt to abide by them and to enforce them. We have seen comparisons with the Victorian era, when efforts by the charities and the educational establishment seemed to work, in turning the quite unbelievably hard world of Dickens into the much better-ordered world of the early twentieth century.

Points to Ponder

Can the law actually solve such behavioural problems?
How would one devise a school programme to cope?
Do our present charities – for child welfare, prison reform and the like – present suitable opportunities for action?

Books to Read:

Konrad Lorenz – King Solomon's Ring – On Aggression
Niko Tinbergen – Social Behaviour in Animals
Robert Ardrey – African Genesis, Hunting Hypothesis, Social Contract, Territorial Imperative

---

ON VOCATION

Before leaving school most children will already have started to think about how they will earn their living in the years ahead. If they are sensible they may already have thought about the subjects that will be needed to be studied and the qualifications they will need to attain. One or two may have been inspired at a very early age – by a relative or a friend, by a teacher or a club leader – to consider but one option, and they pursue that option with all the single-mindedness necessary to achieve their ambition. Even when approaching the time of school leaving others will not yet have even begun to consider what they will need to do: not very farsighted, but not the end of the world either. Whatever they decide, most will be concerned to earn money – to support the desire for fast cars, good clothes, fantastic holidays; or better, it is to be hoped, a little later to support a mate and to bring up a family.

In thinking about future economic activity, it is a good idea to take on board two opposing ideas, which the Germans distinguish with two different words. There is the need to satisfy yourself and your wants – for there is nothing worse than to find yourself stuck in a job which you hate or for which you are simply not qualified; and incidentally nothing better than to be paid to do a job which you adore and would happily do for nothing. Many years ago there was a computer programme which was designed to sort out a suitable job for those undecided: one filled in a sheet detailing qualifications, likes and dislikes, which was then fed into an optical reader; and lo and behold, it then printed out a list of jobs which matched the profile. It was found that sometimes it actually worked; more often it did not, for there are always personal considerations which upset even the canniest of computers. But there is also the need to consider what is best for society – for society has needs also. When I was a student there was even then talk of making university tuition subject to fees – and the outcry was enormous! I suggested then that the Government of the day could indulge in a little social engineering, by waiving the fees for certain courses leading to jobs which were socially necessary: if there was a shortage of nurses, then students wishing to take up nursing could do so free of charge, even if they had to sign an undertaking to work in nursing for a given period of time.

There are certain occupations for which a true sense of "vocation" is needed. Many jobs which society feels are necessary are in fact not very well paid; in addition they are often messy, uncomfortable and even dangerous. For those jobs people need to be "called" in a very real sense and that is after all what that word "vocation" means. It involves sacrifice of time, to become well-trained; of personal comfort; and above all of the chances to earn real money. The days are long gone when we could rely on dedicated amateurs to do these jobs, people who perhaps had private means to see them through. Now we demand, and quite rightly so, properly qualified individuals; even if we are not as a society ready to pay them what they are really worth, they do for the most part at least have a subsistence wage. Many young people, even while still in fill time education, are already showing that due regard for the less fortunate among us, by volunteering for work in hospitals or children's homes, or in mentoring younger people. How many of us can make the extra, very long, step? Are you ready to take up such work full-time? Have you in effect been called to do such work? Are you prepared to make the necessary sacrifices? If so, I wish you well, with all my heart.

Points to Ponder

What do you understand by the term "vocation"?
Do you feel "called" in that sense?
Are you prepared to do what is necessary to follow your "vocation"?
Should we now, as a society, abandon the idea of the gifted amateur in such cases, and instead insist on properly trained and qualified people?

ACKNOWLEDGEMENTS

People too numerous to mention have played a part in shaping the thoughts on which this collection is based – colleagues, friends, pupils, even writers of articles in newspapers and magazines. But more particularly I would like to thank most warmly the Revd Bryn Thomas for his helpful suggestions when this project first seemed likely to get off the ground; and latterly Carol Rogers and her team for their encouragement in getting it all into some coherent form.

Biblical quotations are from the New Revised Standard Version of the Bible © 1989, The Division of Christian Education of the National Council of the Churches of Christ in the United States. Used by permission.

Page 20   (On Death) "If I should go before the rest of you" by Joyce Grenfell (Copyright © Joyce Grenfell Memorial Trust, 1980) is reproduced by permission of Sheil Land Associates Ltd on behalf of the Estate of Joyce Grenfell.

Page 41   (On Harvest Time) God in his love for us lent us this planet by Fred Pratt Green. Reproduced by permission of Stainer & Bell Ltd, London, England.

Page 94   (On Service) "Brother, Sister, let me serve you" by Richard Gillard © Copyright 1977 Scripture in Song (a Div of Integrity Music Inc.) Sovereign Music UK P.O. Box 356, Leighton Buzzard, LU7 3WP UK. Reproduced by permission.

Printed in the United Kingdom
by Lightning Source UK Ltd.
110155UKS00001B/85-282

9 780853 462491